STONES

STONES

An Extraordinary Invitation
to Ordinary People

STEPHEN MCCORMICK

credo
house publishers

Published 2019 in the United States by Credo House Publishers,
a division of Credo Communications LLC, Grand Rapids, Michigan
credohousepublishers.com

All Scripture quotations, unless otherwise indicated, are from the English Standard
Version, Crossway Bibles, a division of Good News Publishers. Wheaton, IL 60187.

ISBN   978-1-625861-29-0

Cover and interior design by Klaas Wolterstorff
Editing by Brent Baker and Donna Huisjen

Cover photo © Stephen McCormick

Printed in the United States of America

First Edition

"When your children ask . . . ,

'What do those stones mean to you?'

then you shall tell them . . ."

JOSHUA 4:6–7

BILL
IN APPRECIATION OF
YOUR FELLOWSHIP!

Steve

Dedication

For my children, grandchildren, and great grandchildren,
for as many generations as follow me and wonder
whether God is real, hears prayer, and answers . . .

You will experience a myriad of opportunities to doubt God, His existence, His interest in the affairs of people, and His awareness of your circumstances. You will have times when nothing makes sense, when continuing on in the journey with the Lord seems to be a waste of time. I know, because I have been there, done that, got the shirt.

But when those times have come in my own life I have remembered the stories you are about to read. They serve as a constant prod for me to keep going; to remain faithful; to know that the One who knows me, and is intimately interested in my life, waits at the end of the path for me. He has left me these sign posts, markers, indicators at the forks in the road, not just to remind me of which way to go but as proof that He has been faithful to do what He first promised me He would do.

I just want you to know that He promises to make Himself known in an intimate way only to those who seek Him with all their hearts. People did not deserve this kind of treatment. We were sinners, enemies of God, when He chose to make a personal relationship with Himself possible.

This book is dedicated also to my father, Gerald McCormick, whose perseverance through the hardships of life has taught me to never give up on that which is hard, but worth the effort. Those shoes have been difficult to fill. The years have not been kind to him, and his path has been difficult. I have witnessed him on numerous occasions come to what would have been the end for the average man, only to rise up, dust himself off, and continue on his journey. He has been an inspiration to me to do the same.

If not for the ministry of Pastor Gail Pike, and his wife, Joan, this book would never have been written. They have both been in the presence of the Lord for several years, and I so wish I could have shared this with them. It was through Pastor Pike that I came to love and revere studying Scripture, and it was through Mrs. Pike that I came to understand the work of the Holy Spirit in my life. Both of them loved me as a son. They were the first to see that God was doing a genuine work in and through my life, and they were my two biggest spiritual cheerleaders. It is impossible for me to overstate how important they were in forming something worthwhile from the train wreck life I had made for myself.

They were more than just examples for us, encouragers at all times, tough when they needed to be. Because of them my wife, Audrey, has remained my faithful life partner through the crazy roller-coaster ride that our lives became in July of 1979. She has had her own journey of transformation since her embrace of Jesus as Savior and Lord in November of that year. It has been amazing to watch her grow from a young woman with no interest in children to a mother of five daughters, and now nine grandchildren.

"Now to him who is able to do far more abundantly than all that we ask or think, according to the power at work within us, to him be glory in the church and in Christ Jesus throughout all generations, forever and ever. Amen." Ephesians 3:20-21

Contents

A Memorial Forever

"Then Joshua called the twelve men from the people of Israel, whom he had appointed, a man from each tribe. And Joshua said to them, 'Pass on before the ark of the LORD your God into the midst of the Jordan, and take up each of you a stone upon his shoulder, according to the number of the tribes of the people of Israel, that this may be a sign among you. When your children ask in time to come, "What do those stones mean to you?" then you shall tell them that the waters of the Jordan were cut off before the ark of the covenant of the LORD. When it passed over the Jordan, the waters of the Jordan were cut off. So these stones shall be to the people of Israel a memorial forever.'" Joshua 4:4-7

In your imagination can you see the last of the 12 men place his stone prominently on top of the heap, an ad hoc memorial pillar to what had just happened? In the years to come, imaginations would be strained to believe what the hand of God had done. The man may have envisioned bringing his own children, and even perhaps his grandchildren, back here to this place. He could see himself telling them the story in front of this pile of stones, pointing to the one he had carried and set in place.

The Jordan River, sometimes little more than a wide stream, was at flood stage, typical for the time of year. It was all that stood between the people of Israel and the land they had been promised through their ancestor, Abraham. Crossing it would be impossible, or so it appeared. But Yahweh used the situation as an opportunity to exalt the leadership of Joshua and to demonstrate God's power and provision. Although His Son would one day walk on water, God chose to part the Jordan for His people to walk through it.

But it was not enough for that generation alone to experience the hand of God moving on their behalf. Yahweh wanted the story preserved for future generations with a visual reminder: a pile of stones removed from the riverbed itself. It would be a testimony of God's direction and intervention in the lives of the people He had set apart for Himself.

The apostle John had that same sense of urgency to make it clear to those who read his writings that the things they had experienced were real, tangible manifestations of the presence and work of God in Jesus. He wrote that the things he recorded in his Gospel were selected so that the readers might believe and have life in Christ. In 1 John he starts his letter by writing:

> "That which was from the beginning, which we have heard, which we have seen with our eyes, which we looked upon and have touched with our hands, concerning the word of life—the life was made manifest, and we have seen it, and testify to it and proclaim to you the eternal life, which was with the Father and was made manifest to us—that which we have seen and heard we proclaim also to you, so that you too may have fellowship with us; and indeed our fellowship is with the Father and with his Son Jesus Christ. And we are writing these things so that our joy may be complete." 1 John 1:1–4

Heard . . . seen . . . touched—the last of the apostles wanted to be sure his readers understood that they had experienced and examined the supernatural made tangible when it came to the question of the Messiah, regardless of what the readers had encountered in their previous religious experiences. Jesus was the real deal, and they knew it without question, with enough certainty to stake their lives on it.

But we live in a world where the supernatural and miraculous, and stories reporting them, are viewed with increasing skepticism or outright rejection. The failure of churches and church leaders has only compounded the problems for those whose faith has been slender to begin with. Increasingly, those in the margins have become the "nones."

At 64 years old, I have much more in common with those less than half my age than they might realize. If the religious demographic term "nones" had existed when I was college age, I would have ticked that box on survey sheets. "Nones" are those who have given up on organized religion for many reasons. A child of parents who had experienced failures of "the church" in my childhood, I wanted nothing to do with what I perceived it to be. Still, I could not escape the reality of a spiritual plane of existence in life.

I would not describe myself as "gifted" in spiritual things prior to 1979. But I would definitely say I was more sensitive to that dimension than any of my friends were. I would know and perceive things that went beyond my natural senses, things for which science and a materialistic view of life did not offer an adequate explanation. I ended up involved in the occult as a result.

But even that involvement in the spiritual plane did not satisfy the longing in my heart for wholeness. Years of broken relationships left me searching for something that made sense of it all, that stopped the whirlpool that was constantly trying to suck me in. It pushed me to the brink of taking my own life to escape the despair and frustration that had accumulated over two and a half decades.

"Church" had done nothing to address that void in my life. Ritual and regulation offered me "pie in the sky by and by" but did nothing about the fact that I was inwardly starving to death in the here and now. If God were there, why couldn't I know that, experientially, in real time? If "God so loved the world" where was the evidence of that affection? This book is about answering those questions. To the "nones" reading these pages I want to say, "Come and see what I found!"

The chapters that follow are the stones of my own memorial pillar, a reminder of the moments when I saw, heard, and experienced what I believe has been the hand of God moving in the details of my life. It is a recounting of the times when I needed and received His intervention, sometimes in specific answer to prayer—and, on occasion, immediately after my engaging in prayer. Some are simply events, the timing of which, or details involved, led me to believe they were the hand of the Lord fulfilling His promise to provide or to direct my footsteps. Coincidence? Perhaps, but I don't think so.

The original purpose of this book was to stand as that pillar for my descendants of that which I have seen, heard, and touched. But there is a further goal for me. My writing is motivated from a desire that people understand that they don't have to have the spiritual stature of a Billy Graham, or a D. L. Moody, to have this kind of interaction with God. I am as average as they come. No one outside my small circle of friends and acquaintances has heard of me.

It is true that my own motivation comes from stories by and about people like the spiritual giants I have mentioned. The belief that God interacts with His people is fueled not only by the pages of Scripture, but from the more recent books on the lives of individuals like George Mueller, who fed thousands in his orphanages in England to prove that God is real; Bruce Olson, who as a teenager was directed into the jungles of South America to reach a Stone-Age tribe known as the Motilones; or Josh McDowell, who as a convicted and converted atheist felt thrust into the jungle of American college campuses to reach its students.

I relished their stories, and those of many other people just like me, who believed in the reality of a personal God and whose lives bore the imprint of that reality. I wanted to be like them. I wanted to know this God, not just theoretically based on ancient stories from a hotly debated book, but practically, in real time, now.

Scripture is to a great extent a collection of God stories, a compilation of firsthand accounts of people who had the same kind of personal interaction with God. To be sure, many of those stories go far beyond anything I have encountered, but, as James reminds us, "Elijah was a human being, even as we are. He prayed earnestly that it would not rain, and it did not rain on the land for three and a half years" (James 5:17 NIV).

But I am getting ahead of myself.

All of the stories you will read happened just as I have written them down, with as much detail as possible. In many cases any people involved in them are still alive to verify their occurrence. In some I have changed the names of the person or persons involved because I could not make contact for permission to use a correct name. A few stories were shared with me as firsthand accounts by those who experienced the events. In the few instances in which I have included their accounts, I have done my best to verify the information. I included them primarily because these stories confirm that I am not the only person who has had similar contemporary experiences when needing God's intervention.

You may struggle to believe some of the stories. That's okay. I would too if they hadn't happened to me. But I didn't write them down for you just to believe them. If you believed every one of them, but that acceptance had no impact on your life, what purpose would that serve?

Instead, I have written them down so that they will produce questions in your mind. How can these things have so consistently occurred in one guy's life? Why would he make all of this up? Why should I care if they happened to him? Why don't I see these kinds of things happening in my life, since I go to church? What would it take for me to start experiencing this kind of personal interaction with God?

I have found it to be easy for people to blow off the stories in the Bible as a gathering of the fables and fantasies of ancient, ignorant people who lived in times of powerful superstition. But while those stories may be easily dismissed by unbelievers because they cannot be verified, it can be unnerving for them to hear contemporary accounts of God's interaction with His people when the effects can be seen. This is consistent with the ministry of Jesus, when crowds were drawn to Him because of the way God manifested His presence in validation of what Jesus taught. He tried to win their ears for the gospel message by gaining their awed attention (John 10:37-38).

I know I am not the only one to whom things like these are happening. I have brothers and sisters in Christ who have told me stories from their own lives that make mine pale in comparison.

I cannot coerce you (nor would I want to do so) to believe in a personal God who interacts with His children. I can only tell you what happened after I believed in Him and hope that the lack of any reasonable explanation for these events other than the existence and interaction of God challenges what you, the reader, may already hold to be true.

One of my daughters, Allison, as a child once asked one of the most astute questions I have ever had posed to me. We had just shared in a devotional, or informal Bible study, in the backyard. We were walking back to the house when she asked, "But how do you know that what you believe is the truth?" I was astonished by her sincerity and the weight of the question. How would you have answered it?

I know because I have not only read the things written in Scripture by those who "heard, and saw, and touched" the reality of what they passed on, but I have heard and seen and touched the reality of God's involvement in my own life many times. As I have often said, I simply don't have enough faith to be an atheist. There is not a single belief system in the entire religious universe that offers me what I have encountered as a disciple of Jesus.

A person does not need to be famous, or powerful, or even saintly to experience the presence and power of God. You just need to be an obedient disciple of Jesus.

Notice, I said obedient. I didn't say a perfect disciple, or a mature disciple, or an ascetic disciple. If those were the requirements, I could not have written this book, because I have struggled in my walk as a disciple, just as those earliest disciples did.

And it is Jesus' selection of spiritual nobodies as the first disciples that gave me hope and encouragement to be a follower and to personally encounter God.

Discipleship involves disciplines, true, but it is not self-abandonment to a list of *dos* and *don'ts*. Principles in Scripture serve a primary purpose of helping us to engage God on a daily basis, to know his provision, direction, and affection.

The stories in this book are the result of applying those principles to real life situations. If I find there is interest I may compile those principles of effective prayer in a future publication. In it all my hope is that you, the reader, will be impressed not by the author of this book but the Author of the Book. I didn't dream all of this up on my own, and I am no one special. I read His book and, in doing so, made an amazing discovery.

He has extended an extraordinary invitation to ordinary people.

CHAPTER 1

His Story

"**Y**ou have got to read this book!" I didn't know it at the time my wife said it, but she was right. And neither of us had any idea how profoundly that reading would change our lives.

My wife, Audrey, essentially a book junkie, was getting her current literary fix from one of Stephen King's books, *The Stand*. It was nothing unusual to see her with a book in her hands, but I had never seen her with this kind of a reaction to a work of fiction.

Still, I had little interest in reading. I was an activity-oriented guy. Tennis, biking, running, and especially theater absorbed all my free time. There was one thing I didn't have any time for: God. Why should I? When I needed Him He never seemed to be available.

I remember lying in bed one night as a child, sobbing. "God, if you are there, why don't you do something?"

Our family life was a disaster. One brother was killed as a toddler by a drunk driver, and my parents would not emotionally recover from that for decades. My dad lost his electrical contracting business over a bad decision he made trying to help his employees. Bill collectors called incessantly as my dad struggled to fulfill his commitment to pay off everyone to whom he owed money rather than declare bankruptcy.

My parents' marriage teetered on divorce year after year as they tried to blend two "oil and water" cultures. Mom was prim and proper, having attended convent school in England. Dad grew up the youngest child of a poor rural family in Michigan, embarrassed to wear his worn-out, hand-me-down clothes in front of other students.

I had been raised in a mainline denominational church, complete with catechism and confirmation. But during my later teen years my family no longer attended church. As a result of some high school experiences I became involved in the occult, leading to active involvement in reading tarot cards and palms and experimenting with mental telepathy, ESP, and the like. I was well acquainted with, and interested in, a spiritual aspect of life, but at that point it had nothing to do with God.

My previous church experience had been a "Sunday only" encounter. My religious training classes, while informative, had focused on death rather than life, the next world and not this one. There was nothing ever taught about a personal relationship with God. He was just out there somewhere, mostly keeping score for the big day. It seemed as though, as far as life was concerned, we were pretty much on our own, and that was all the freedom I needed to make a real mess out of mine.

In July of 1979, my life was at the bottom of the barrel. I was 25, depressed for months at a time, and searching desperately for something to fill the void in my heart. I was cheating on my wife; stealing at work; and getting stoned literally morning, noon, and at night. Profanity was my second language.

It was then that my wife read *The Stand*. The black hole in my life was sucking in everything around it and letting nothing back out. I was spinning out of control, and I began to fear what would happen if I didn't make some kind of change. But what? What had to change? I began to wonder if the concept behind the character of Mother Abigail in *The Stand* held the answer to my question. She would seek the Lord in prayer, and He would answer her. I knew the book was fiction, but I remember thinking King had to have based her on reality.

Could you actually talk to God and have Him respond?

I was tired of trying to climb out of the hole I had mostly dug myself. Two guys I worked with, Neil Girke and Gary Lounsberry, had something (really, Someone) in their lives I wanted. They never overtly talked about their faith with me, but I could see that something was different, and I knew they both went to a country church a few miles south of where I lived.

So one night I called their pastor, Gail Pike, and went to his office, perhaps as Nicodemus had done some two thousand years earlier. Pastor Pike asked all kinds of questions to determine what I knew about God, Jesus, and sin. I could "dot the *Is* and cross the *Ts*" for everything he asked. He finally stopped me and said, "Steve, I can't believe how much you know, but you don't understand." Then he simply and clearly presented the gospel and asked, "Would you like to receive Jesus as your Lord and Savior?"

I thought about what he had said to me and what a mess my life was, and I said no.

Up to that moment, sitting across that desk, I had never read on my own initiative so much as a page of the Bible. So there was no way I could intellectually know that his question, and my answer, would affect my life beyond anything I could then imagine.

Jesus had promised to make His followers fishers of men, and you could see that in Pastor Pike's eyes as he reeled me in, . . . and as the line snapped.

"Why!?" I never again saw Pastor Pike so astonished or animated. "You have the biggest God-sized, God-shaped hole in your life of anyone I have ever shared the gospel with. Why wouldn't you want to receive Jesus?"

"Because," I said, "I went through the motions once as a teenager, prayed a prayer, and it made no difference in my life. I am not interested in that." I thought about what I had learned in all those classes, again with no effect on my life. "But from what you have told me tonight, if I embrace this it will change my life. I want to be sure I am ready for it." And I left.

"Then Jesus told his disciples, 'If anyone would come after me, let him deny himself and take up his cross and follow me. For whoever would save his life will lose it, but whoever loses his life for my sake will find it.'" Matthew 16:24–25

Not once in all my religious training had anyone told me that. Take up and let go. I had no knowledge of "the cost of discipleship," at least none that I am aware of. My teachers had never talked about this in all the classes I had attended growing up. Either instinctively, or because the Holy Spirit revealed it to me, I somehow knew that everything about my life could change. Two weeks later, after sitting through two more messages under Pastor Pike, I also knew that I had no other option. I asked Jesus to save me on the way home from church.

From that moment on my life turned upside down. No, I didn't have a car wreck, but the effect of that prayer was just as dramatic. As clichéd as this may sound, it was one of those "I was dead, but now I live—was blind but now I see" events. I don't know how else to describe it. On the way to church a few weeks later I remember turning to my wife in the car, saying, "This is crazy. It's like I have gone to another planet! I didn't know people lived like this."

I went from no interest in God to no interest in anything else. Like a starving man at a smorgasbord I devoured Scripture, staying up late night after night to read. It was then that I began to understand from the Gospels what discipleship was about. I had found the personal relationship with Jesus for which I had been longing and looking without realizing it. "If anyone would come after me . . ." included *me*. It could be no more personal than that.

Stephen King's book had sparked the question, but now The King's Book was answering it. One of the first things Jesus' disciples had asked Him to do was teach them to pray (Matthew 6:9). I wanted the same thing. I began to see patterns and principles of prayer in the Bible. Nearly everything that follows has been the result.

I discovered the most basic laws of the kingdom: He called—I followed; I called—He fulfilled.

His story became my story. I was no longer a "none."

I had become a son.

CHAPTER 2

Out of the Blue

"**D**oes Steve have any camera equipment for sale?" There was no way my wife could possibly have known the question from one of her coworkers would be a precise answer to my first prayer experiment, setting a pattern for the rest of my life.

A spiritual tsunami had swept over me. Getting high had been a focal point of my life. No one had told me I had to stop getting stoned after I came to faith in Christ—I just knew. I pitched the smoking paraphernalia and flushed the grass down the toilet. Being involved in theater, both as an actor and as a director, had dominated my life for ten years, but the need evaporated, and I was never involved with another production. I had never been able to stop swearing, but suddenly my tongue was free and the profanity ceased. I had been to counselors repeatedly for the emotional distress in my life, with no lasting change. The Lord had done almost overnight what psychologists had failed to do in years.

Even though I had been saved for only a few months, I had started hearing and reading lots of missionary stories about God intervening in people's lives in surprising ways. Something inside longed to know if God would do the same thing in my life. I wanted to see what would happen if I began to trust Him as these others did. And one thing was my highest priority: I wanted to know how to talk to God so He would respond. I knew I needed to learn how to pray.

The Old and New Testaments abound with stories of God interacting with His chosen people. Sometimes it is simply in the direction of events surrounding their lives, but in others it is in specific answers to prayer. In that respect nothing is so striking as the last interaction Jesus had with His disciples before the crucifixion, as recorded in the Gospel of John, chapters 14–16.

In these chapters, Jesus spoke to His disciples about the responsibility they would have after He was gone. The phrase "in my name" appears seven times, referring in each to an official relationship. It is that of a representative or agent charged with what would be referred to as "power of attorney" in modern terminology. The agent conducts business or the affairs "in the name" of someone not physically present. The phrase "in Jesus' name" is not simply a catchy Christian addendum to tack on to giving thanks for lunch. It is the means to seek and accomplish the Lord's will in His kingdom.

I so clearly remember my first lesson on this subject and the application of this principle to my own life.

I had been doing freelance photography for a few years before I was saved, particularly for the local paper. It was fun to see my work published on a fairly regular basis.

But after I came to faith in Christ I sensed my priorities beginning to change. I found less and less time I was willing to spend in my darkroom processing images. I had accumulated exactly what I wanted for darkroom equipment, especially my Beseler 23C II enlarger, my pride and joy. But my heart pulled me in a different direction now, and I started to feel conflicted about how much money I had tied up in equipment I wasn't using.

There is nothing intrinsically wrong with photography, or hobbies in general, for that matter. I am not saying that following Jesus requires giving up all personal possessions, especially something that could be used directly for the Lord. But my heart wasn't in it for that season, and I didn't know what to do. I needed wisdom.

I decided it was time to begin to ask God for one of the things

Scripture promised he would give—wisdom. *Wisdom* is a doing word. It is about choices, and following through on them. I had never asked God to guide a personal decision before, so it felt pretty awkward for the first experience. Did I really believe God cared whether or not I had a darkroom?

Would God guide me in even small decisions if I asked for it? I reminded Him of the promise to provide wisdom, as I read it in James 1:5-8:

> "If any of you lacks wisdom, let him ask God, who gives generously to all without reproach, and it will be given him. But let him ask in faith, with no doubting, for the one who doubts is like a wave of the sea that is driven and tossed by the wind. For that person must not suppose that he will receive anything from the Lord; he is a double-minded man, unstable in all his ways."

I tried to make sure it was actually God involved in the decision, in more or less the same manner as Gideon had done with the fleece (Judges 6:36-40). I could totally relate to Gideon: I wanted to try to be sure it was not me imagining or manipulating the situation.

I didn't tell anyone what I was praying for but asked God whether I should sell the darkroom equipment—asked Him, if His answer was affirmative, to have someone come up out of the blue and ask if I had any photography equipment for sale. I made the answer to prayer I was looking for difficult, but in no way impossible. I was not trying to avoid selling the equipment, just trying to make sure that if God had a purpose and plan in mind I wouldn't miss it.

A few days later my wife came home from a pharmacy in town. "Jerry Richlich [one of the guys she worked with] came up to me in the store and asked if you have any photography equipment for sale. I told him I didn't know. He wants you to call him. Do you have any for sale?" I was stunned.

At first I couldn't believe what seemed to be happening. I had known Jerry for years. We were both members of the local theater group, The Community Players. He had never before expressed any interest in my photography equipment.

Then I started coming up with reasons this couldn't be an answer to my prayer. Jerry hadn't come up to *me* and asked. But I hadn't asked for that in my prayer. He hadn't specified darkroom equipment to Audrey. But again, I hadn't specified asking about darkroom equipment.

The more ideas I came up with as reasons to dismiss what had happened, the more the warning in James 1:6–8 goaded me:

> "But when you ask, you must believe and not doubt, because the one who doubts is like a wave of the sea, blown and tossed by the wind. That person should not expect to receive anything from the Lord. Such a person is double-minded and unstable in all they do." (NIV)

I didn't want to be that person.

I had asked God to give me wisdom about what to do. If I backed out now by splitting hairs, would I ever see God direct the course of my life, as I hoped? Would I ever see bigger, genuine, specific answers to prayer? I decided I had to call Jerry.

"I have been thinking about selling my darkroom equipment, but no camera gear," I told him. I was too embarrassed to tell him about the prayer. "Great!" he said, "That's what I'm looking for." And he bought my whole darkroom outfit. I gained something in the deal I hadn't had before, something money can't buy.

For the first time I experienced what the apostle Paul refers to in Philippians 4:7: "And the peace of God, which surpasses all understanding, will guard your hearts and your minds in Christ Jesus." Verse 6 in that passage indicates that this is a peace that results from making your requests known to God and then trusting Him to act in a manner consistent with His will on the matter. Peace surpassing all understanding is a peace that cannot be rationally explained. I had peace knowing that I had involved God in the process and that He had given me wisdom about what to do.

The darkroom equipment was gone, and the empty closet stood as a reminder. But the anxiety over having so much money tied up in equipment I wasn't using was also gone. I thought I would miss working in the darkroom, but God wasn't finished with me on that issue.

A few years later the Lord would direct me into a position as a photographer for a ministry, and they had a darkroom with the same equipment I had sold. I had the pleasure of doing darkroom work again, but with no lingering question mark hanging over me. Instead of the possibility that activity was a waste of my time and money, or hindering my walk with the Lord, He was enabling me to use it for establishing His kingdom.

And that is the base on which Jesus taught His disciples to establish their prayer lives.

CHAPTER 3

Do Not Grieve

I opened the door of the restaurant and quickly scanned the occupants. Then he caught my eye, the old man at the counter on the swivel stool. "Oh, no, Lord . . . not him!" And I sensed the presence of the Lord about to leave me in the doorway.

So much in those early months of my walk with the Lord had been so radically different from anything I had experienced before. Much of what hindered me in life had changed immediately—but not everything. There was much about myself, about wrong attitudes and actions, that would take time to discover and deal with.

One of the classic mistakes about Christianity is to see it as a list of *dos* and *don'ts* as religious formalities to practice. At the same time, it is clear from the teachings of Jesus that entering the kingdom of God as a disciple requires leaving an old lifestyle to enter a new one. But "to-do lists" hadn't worked so well with the chosen people of God, the nation of Israel, under their old Mosaic covenant. So He promised them a new relationship with Himself. Instead of leaving them with commandments written on stone and scrolls, He would write them on their hearts.

Every disciple of Jesus receives a gift, the indwelling Holy Spirit, to reside in them and guide them in the path each should follow. The personal relationship with God I had sought was even more personal than I had imagined. Jesus had promised that indwelling in John 14:15–26 and had indicated that the Holy Spirit would take up the discipling role in Jesus' place.

In practical terms, this meant that Jesus would no longer be limited to teaching one small group of disciples in one location, as He had done for three years in Israel. Instead, He would live in them by the presence of the Holy Spirit and disciple them, wherever and whenever that was needed.

Although I had been sensitive to the spiritual dimension of life prior to becoming a follower of Jesus, this relationship went far beyond anything I had previously experienced. I slowly became aware of and accustomed to the prompting of the Holy Spirit as I began the transition from walking in the flesh to walking under the influence and direction of the Spirit. I was seeking to develop this new relationship more fully and completely in my new life when one event drove home its importance to me.

I really had no idea how selfish I was being in my relationships with other people. The Lord began to walk me through seeking forgiveness for the wrongs I had done to others, and one by one my conscience was cleansed from those past actions. I also began evaluating my current interactions with people through a new filter. And I was discovering the patterns of thought that led to wrong actions. They had to go as well.

Returning to my opening story, one day I was heading into a coffee shop in Allegan, my hometown, and I prayed just before I grasped the door knob: "When I open the door, God, indicate someone I should sit and talk with, if possible, sharing Jesus with that person." I had no idea the Holy Spirit was about to turn this into a teachable moment for me, perhaps even more than to the one I would speak with.

As I opened the door I quickly scanned the room of 15 or so customers. There were a few about my age, but eventually my eyes were drawn to an old man sitting at the counter by himself. In an instant I knew this was the one the Lord wanted me to speak to. But my reaction was not exactly spiritual.

"Oh no, Lord, not him!"

Let me be quick to say that there was nothing wrong with the man, and that I had no negative history with him. In fact, I knew him only by sight and name. But, well, he was "old." I was about to discover that my sharing of the Lord with others was far too much about me and not about the person with whom I was sharing. I expected that any conversation we might have would be, for lack of a better word, boring.

I did know one thing further. This man attended the same church in which I had grown up, and with which I wanted nothing more to do. This conversation could be awkward.

The apostle Paul warned his readers, "Do not grieve the Holy Spirit of God, by whom you were sealed for the day of redemption" (Ephesians 4:30). The Holy Spirit can be grieved and offended by our words and actions. I was about to find out how sensitive the Spirit is.

As soon as the thought formed in my mind, I could sense the Holy Spirit grieving within me. It was as though I could hear the Spirit say, "Okay, sit with whomever you like, but I'm out of here." The presence of the Lord that was so new to me began to fade. "No, Lord! I will sit with him!"

I sat at the counter beside him and struck up a conversation, eventually steering it in a spiritual direction. And then something totally unexpected happened. I discovered that he was as passionate about his relationship with the Lord as I was. We sat at the counter and had great fellowship over my break.

As I left the restaurant, I felt as though I were walking about six inches above the sidewalk, in part because of the fellowship but mostly because I had obeyed the Holy Spirit's prompting and sensed His blessing on that obedience. The Holy Spirit wanted to minister to both of us, and my hard heart had indeed grieved Him.

There was an even more important lesson for me in this meeting. It was the discovery that even in churches that have problems, and even in whole denominations that may be struggling and/or declining, there are still believers who are passionate about their relationship with Jesus. It is the church—not Jesus—that often fails and offends the "nones," driving them away just as it had myself and my family.

The Bible is full of examples of God's presence, even in the midst of rebellious people. He was at work in the midst of Israel through the prophets even when the people had stopped following Yahweh. Jesus was active in the midst of the nation even when the leadership was failing to perceive and follow.

I believe the Holy Spirit set that up as a divine appointment, and the importance of the lesson was not lost on me.

CHAPTER 4

Hide and Seek

"And they heard the sound of the LORD God walking in the garden in the cool of the day, and the man and his wife hid themselves from the presence of the LORD God among the trees of the garden." Genesis 3:8

I had been seeking God with my whole heart, and obeying as soon as I was aware of His leading. As I was praying one day, I suddenly became aware of a presence in the room, and it frightened me. All my years of involvement in the occult had not prepared me for what I was experiencing about a year after becoming a Christian.

In high school I had developed an interest in the paranormal. In psychology class I had paired up with a cousin who was completely freaked out by my ability to sense things she was experiencing. She abruptly ended the experiment and refused to continue. To me that was no big deal.

I eventually started reading tarot cards and palms, and I actually became pretty good at predicting things. But after I was saved I wanted to break away from communication with spirits. It wasn't easy or automatic. I reached a point at which I could sense them waking me up at night, trying to pull me back into that kind of involvement with the spirit realm. I finally decided I had to talk with an assistant pastor from our church.

Don took the information in stride. "The next time it happens, call me, regardless of what time it is." I told him I would, and took him at his word a few nights later when this occurred again. I called him in the middle of the night, and after he had gotten his wits about him he prayed, taking authority over the powers of darkness. That was the end of the middle-of-the-night contacts.

About that time God brought another brother in Christ, Brett Strong, into my life to help me become more aware of what I had gotten myself into with my occult involvement, how to break free, and how to stay free from spiritual bondage.

In all my occult experiences I had never felt fear—only curiosity and thrill at being involved with the supernatural. I didn't notice the constant din of thoughts running through my head, regarding them simply as my own. When I later went through a deliverance session with an itinerant evangelist, Tom Harmon, they abruptly stopped. This was the first time I had experienced a quiet mind from as far back as I could remember.

But learning to be sensitive to the prompting and presence of God was another story. About a year after I had received Christ as Savior, I realized I was starting to flirt with my former interests and lifestyle prior to being saved. As I allowed that to happen, I realized I was becoming distant from the Lord, and it scared me to think of returning to what my life had been.

"Please, God," I cried out, lying facedown on the living room floor, "Please don't let me go back. I don't care what it costs to go forward, but please don't let me go back." A peace came over me that I sensed was from the Lord, confirming that he would not allow me to slip back into the bondage and despair of my former life.

Some time later—days or weeks, I'm not sure—I was worshiping and seeking the Lord once again in my living room, where I had previously prayed on my face. I suddenly became aware of an increasingly intense spiritual presence in the room.

I am not sure whether that is what Scripture refers to as holy fear, an awesome reverence for God, but it was overwhelming. It wasn't as though I was afraid God would harm me, but more that I was afraid in the sense Peter, James, and John must have been on the Mount of Transfiguration coming into contact with something they had no ability to understand (Matthew 17:1–8; Mark 9:2–8). As I read the verses, I can only conjecture that these disciples must have passed out from fear. There was no visible manifestation in my room, as they had experienced, but the presence was just as real as anything I had ever encountered.

I was not part of a charismatic or Pentecostal congregation, and I had no frame of reference for what was happening. I'll have to admit that I panicked, just as Peter had, and blurted the first thing that came to mind: "Lord, I can't handle this! I need to ask you to back away."

The sense of the presence rapidly diminished, and I have regretted ever since having spoken so rashly. Moments after it was gone, I remember saying, "I don't care what happens, but I will never pray that again."

God promised that even if His people had lost their connection with Yahweh through disobedience, there was a way they could find Him again: "But from there you will seek the LORD your God and you will find him, if you search after him with all your heart and with all your soul" (Deuteronomy 4:29).

One of the most important biblical principles for "nones" to remember is that there is a way home to the Father.

And He is waiting . . .

CHAPTER 5

The Least of These

I was painting the outside of my house one day, and I was angry. Mundane tasks are a good way to find time to pray, and I needed to pray. I had built close relationships with several growing Christians for fellowship and had enjoyed my time with them. Then, in quick succession, and based on varying circumstances, each had been removed from my life.

I have never been an advocate of "yelling at God," as some advise, but I was probably as close that day as I have ever been. Why was God allowing, or even causing, this to happen? Didn't I need encouragement to keep going and growing in my relationship with Jesus?

"Every time I get close to someone for fellowship you take them away!" I almost wanted to throw paint at the house. Even though I wasn't looking for a response, I got one anyway.

"But you aren't seeking *me*."

There wasn't a harsh or condemning tone associated with the thought. It was that of a grieved friend. My anger melted away.

It was true. I suddenly realized I was slowly replacing my relationship with Jesus with interactions and encouragement from other people. Fellowship with likeminded believers is good, but not when it replaces intimacy with the Lord. I had no idea how prone I was to assign rock-star status to people, and in the process get off track spiritually.

I was amazed at the faith displayed by so many in those days when walking with God was new to me. The effect was magnified by those who were my contemporaries. One of the best known in the eighties was Joni Eareckson Tada.

The movie and book about her life after she became paralyzed in a diving accident left a deep impression on me. I was overwhelmed by the tenacity of her faith and trust in God, even though she was not healed of her broken spine and remained a quadriplegic from her shoulders down, confined to a wheelchair for the rest of her life.

When I heard a radio advertisement of a conference featuring Joni in Grand Rapids, Michigan, I determined I had to be there. Seating was going to be limited because of the venue, so I got a ticket early.

The conference was on ministering to the needs of mentally and physically disabled persons, so naturally there were many of them in attendance, along with their caregivers. In so many ways they fit the category Jesus spoke of as "the least of these." I participated in a number of sessions, but, truth be told, I was really at the conference for one primary reason—the possibility of meeting Joni.

She was not involved with any of the sessions in which I participated, but as the keynote speaker she was in the main conference room between sessions. I came into the room a bit late, in the middle of an announcement by the emcee, with Joni in her wheelchair behind him. He said, ". . . As her van pulled into the parking deck the alternator belt broke, and we are wondering if anyone here has tools and could help her." Was I dreaming?

Although I was not a licensed mechanic, I worked on vehicles all the time. I just happened to have my tools in my car. Could it be true that I was going to get to repair Joni's vehicle? I quickly got out of my seat to move to the front of the auditorium before anyone else could beat me to the opportunity of a lifetime. I virtually floated to the front of the room.

I stepped to the edge of the platform and introduced myself to the emcee. "I heard your announcement about the broken fan belt, and I have my tools with me. I would like to help." I was excited, so I tried to calm down and prepared to meet Joni. I didn't want to embarrass myself like a complete idiot. As it turned out, I couldn't avoid the idiot part after all.

Instead of turning to Joni, the emcee said, "Great! She is right back there on the aisle seat." I had missed the first part of the announcement. I remember almost falling backward as his arm extended over my head, and I followed it all the way to the end of his finger, which pointed to a young handicapped woman seated almost where I had been sitting. My countenance fell . . . and so did the paddle . . .

The Holy Spirit took the verses I had been memorizing and whacked my spiritual behind:

> "My brothers, show no partiality as you hold the faith in our Lord Jesus Christ, the Lord of glory. For if a man wearing a gold ring and fine clothing comes into your assembly, and a poor man in shabby clothing also comes in, and if you pay attention to the one who wears the fine clothing and say, 'You sit here in a good place,' while you say to the poor man, 'You stand over there,' or, 'Sit down at my feet,' have you not then made distinctions among yourselves and become judges with evil thoughts?" James 2:1–4

Joni had been the favored one I had wanted to impress. The disabled "poor woman" was someone I hadn't even noticed. Then the weight of how evil my thoughts were hit me harder than any woodshed "whuppin" could have. I was excited to help Joni but wasn't concerned for "the least of these" who needed my ability. I was instantly ashamed of what the Lord had revealed in my motives. God disciplines those He loves as sons. This chastening was for my good and His glory.

Without realizing it I was repeating the same mistake that had produced frustration in my life before I had come to know the Lord. I was trying to find my delight in circumstances that fulfilled my desires rather than in Him. Doing so would ultimately set me up for failure—and for blaming that failure on God. David understood the right perspective when he wrote, "Take delight in the LORD, and he will give you the desires of your heart" (Psalm 37:4 NIV). This is another key reason people end up in the "nones" category. We make really selfish choices and blame the consequences on God.

I repented and introduced myself to the young lady. It never occurred to me as we planned to meet after the conference that most of the parts stores would be closed by then. I chased all over Grand Rapids that evening and finally found the belt she needed. I installed it and sent her on her way.

The experience at the conference made me aware of my own disability. It was a debilitating hindrance to my walk with the Lord, an invisible, spiritual one that made me walk with a limp I couldn't see. Turned out the Holy Spirit was my keynote speaker, and the session was tailor made for my particular chronic condition. I wish I could say that I was totally healed that evening. In reality, I have had to seek the Healer repeatedly as I detect that limp in my walk again and again.

It was good to be the instrument for meeting the need of the young woman, but my change of perspective was, for me at least, the best result that came of the incident. I knew the Lord was in it and that it was the right thing to do. Still, I was disappointed that there had been no opportunity at the conference to tell Joni how much her testimony meant to me as a young Christian. But the Lord hadn't written the last paragraph of this God story.

A few years later I heard that Joni was returning to Grand Rapids, this time to the Calvin College campus. I remembered what I had learned about not applying "rock-star" status to servants of God, even to someone with the high profile Joni had in the Christian community. Still, the principles she brought out from application of the Scriptures to her circumstances of life were powerful, and I wanted to hear what she had to say. But this time I would not make the same mistake.

The lesson the Lord had taught me was still fresh in my mind. To safeguard against giving in to a wrong motive, I determined beforehand that I would not attempt to meet her. I got there early and chose a spot about four rows up on the low bleacher seating, as close to the exit as possible so I could leave quickly.

As hundreds of people gathered to listen to her, I thought about the impact of someone surrendered to the will of the Lord, even if it was a difficult path to walk. I wanted that same kind of trust in God's plan, whatever that might mean for me.

The room darkened as the time drew near for her to come to the platform, and the emcee began to address the crowd. As I listened, I suddenly became aware of a handicapped woman in a wheelchair on the floor near my feet. I looked closer. Even from above her in the darkness there was no mistaking her identity. It was Joni, waiting to be introduced to the crowd.

She was so close I could have laid my hand on top of her head. I had only seconds to think. I can't imagine what it would be like to be a quadriplegic in a darkened room, and to unexpectedly hear your name whispered from somewhere overhead. If possible, I suspect she might have jumped from her chair as I whispered her name. Startled, she looked up at me. "Thanks so much for your testimony," was all I could think of to say. She smiled before scooting her motorized wheelchair onto the platform to speak.

Joni meets tens of thousands of people every year, and I haven't the slightest reason to believe she remembers that moment. But I have never forgotten that particular instance when God honored His Word. I chose to delight myself in the Lord instead of trying to meet her. I believe the Lord honored that by bringing her to me.

There is one more risk in all of this that drives people into the "nones" category. When we elevate people to pedestals, they tend to fall off. Pastors, speakers, and mentors are all just people, sinners like ourselves. When they do tumble or stumble we may allow disappointment to justify our abandoning church—or even the Lord Himself.

I know from personal experience that disappointments like these leave wounds, bruises, and even scars. Be careful not to blame the Lord for the failings of people, especially when you have elevated them to a place only He deserves in your life.

CHAPTER 6

It's Time to Go

When I came to faith in Christ as my Savior, I was like a starving man led to a banquet table. I devoured Scripture, staying up late into many evenings reading. This was so abnormal for me. My lack of interest in reading evaporated. But I discovered that something else had changed too.

A desire to share that which I learned with others soon surfaced. In all the years I had been a "churched kid," I had never had any sense that I needed to tell anyone else about God or my faith. Now I couldn't stop telling people about what had happened in my life. Within months Pastor Pike figured out that God had given me a gift for preaching and teaching. That assessment was affirmed by small congregations to which he sent me out for pulpit supply. But while I had been given the gift, I sorely needed to develop the skill to go with it.

Soon I found myself wanting to go to Bible school so I could learn to study, preach, and teach more effectively. Something else happened about then that dramatically impacted the direction in my spiritual journey.

Christians in our church talked about having a "life verse." In fact, I heard a lot of references to such verses early on in my walk with the Lord. I thought this was just something I was supposed to do, like a rite of passage. There were a number of verses that seemed important to me as I read the Bible.

Many people I knew gravitated to Proverbs 3:5-6: "Trust in the LORD with all your heart, and do not lean on your own understanding. In all your ways acknowledge him, and he will make straight your paths." These words are a concise statement of an important concept. I liked them, so I adopted them as my life verses—but honestly, inside I somehow knew they weren't the right ones. Although they would be an important part of my spiritual journey, I didn't realize the Lord would give me the one that would mean much more to me personally.

During the late summer of 1980, though I don't remember the exact circumstances, I was plowing through Hebrews when I came across a verse that stopped me and gripped me unlike any others up to that point. When it happened, I felt as though God were teaching me personally about how He was going to lead me. After all I had heard about life verses, I immediately knew this was mine.

Hebrews 11 is often referred to as the Faith Hall of Fame. When I got to verse 8 I was riveted as I read: "By faith Abraham obeyed when he was called to go out to a place that he was to receive as an inheritance. And he went out, not knowing where he was going." The earlier chapters of Hebrews I had been reading had been interesting up to that point, but this was somehow one of those "holy ground moments" like the one Moses had experienced (Exodus 3:5). I imagined what it must be like to take a journey like the one Abram made, without knowing either the destination or what he might encounter along the way. Abram's expectation must have been that God would direct his very steps.

I realized that Scripture was doing more than informing me how God got Abram to Canaan. God was showing me what His guidance of my new life in Christ would look like. He wasn't going to let me see way down the road and make plans of my own on how to get where I was going. He would show me one step at a time—a step of faith that, when taken, would lead to another step to be taken in obedience. I would later learn that when David wrote in Psalm

119:105 "Your word is a lamp to my feet and a light to my path," he was actually describing the function of a foot lamp. It gave just enough light for a person to safely take one step in the pitch darkness, but no more than one.

A sense of awe came over me. I had specifically come to Christ looking for a God who sees, hears, and responds to His people. That the God of the universe would take that kind of interest in me was overwhelming beyond anything I could ever have expected. He had called me to faith in Himself for both the present and eternity, and now he would lead, without my knowing how we would get where He wanted us.

The words essentially gushed out of me when I shared this insight with a group of college-age young adults from our church at a bonfire one night on our property. The sense of amazement at understanding God's active interest in my life was something I would hang on to in the months ahead, as the journey began with turns in the road I would not have chosen if I had been able to see ahead.

My times of reading Scripture became increasingly important to me. I also learned that I needed to be memorizing and meditating on verses that seemed particularly important to the path on which God had set my feet. The more I learned and applied to my life, the more I saw God respond in amazing ways.

Frequent opportunities to preach and teach fueled my desire to go on in school. Every once in a while someone would come along and throw a can of gasoline on the smoldering fire—like a missionary couple who came to our home for dinner. Hearing of my desire to go to school to learn to study, preach, and teach, they promised to pray that God would open the door. I was grateful and impressed with their affirmation.

My wife was not.

Only a few years earlier, before I had been saved, we had for the second time been on the verge of divorce. Audrey came to faith four months later. Same Lord, same faith, . . . but very different experiences. I had been looking for something all my life, something to fill the insatiable black hole in my heart that swallowed up everything I tossed in. For me, salvation was a death-to-life happening, one of those "lost but now I'm found . . . blind but now I see" events. I knew I had found what I had been looking for. I knew I had to change. I hurtled forward full tilt after becoming a Christian.

Audrey and I were as different as night and day. But with regard to spiritual things, we had one thing in common. Neither of us had any interest in the religious training we had received as children.

She started reading the Bible after I had come to trust in Jesus, in part, perhaps, to figure out what had happened to me. She reluctantly came to church with me, essentially because she didn't want to go through a divorce. She got to the book of Revelation, and it scared her so badly she knew she wanted to ask for forgiveness in Christ. But she really didn't see herself as "all that bad"—and compared to me she wasn't.

The aspect of the situation I didn't see was my tendency to go after everything new with the same "jump into the deep end" abandonment. Audrey was afraid this might just be another one of those "been there, done that, got the shirt" events. In the 18 months since my accepting Christ we had pulled back from the brink of divorce, gained some stability in life, and bought a home of our own. She wasn't interested in any more drama, thank you very much. My comments about wanting to go to Bible school sounded to her ears like something akin to my characteristic "Someday I would like to travel to Mars" expressions. "This too shall pass" was her inward mantra. But it didn't.

A subtle tension began to slowly build between us from 1980 to 1983, until once again our relationship was being threatened. I began to see my wife as a hindrance to the fulfillment of my manifest destiny as a great preacher. My hints at going to school were met with comments expressing increasing frustration on her part, and I responded with increasing frustration of my own. I decided to ratchet up the pressure. We both loved and respected our pastor and his wife. I opted to recruit their help in persuading Audrey of God's purpose in my life. My pastor's reaction, though, was not quite as enthusiastic as I had expected.

"I don't think God wants you at Bible school." No, *really*, pastor, tell me what you think. For someone who was loath to tell me specifics about following God's direction in life, this was as subtle as getting hit with a ball bat.

"What do you mean?" I blurted out, stunned by his answer. How could my pastor not believe that God would want me to go to Bible school? Wasn't that like—blasphemy or something?

"When God wants you in Bible school he will call Audrey too. She doesn't want to go. I don't believe it is God's timing for you to go to Bible school now."

"Well, how will I know when it is?" I swear I almost whined. I was against the ropes now, desperate for my spiritual Mike Tyson to miss with the next punch.

"I can't tell you that. But when it's time, you will know." That was it. I was *KO*'d. I don't know how else to describe how I felt. I had been so sure. Now, not only was the wind gone from my sails, but I was sitting on a beach on Gilligan's Island.

What I didn't realize was that in his wise perspective my pastor could see that I was still as insensitive to Audrey as I had always been, only this time blaming it on "God's leading" in my life. It was the same basic type of insensitivity that had been undermining our marriage for years, dressed up in a Sunday suit. God was going to break me of this before he could use me—or, more correctly, use us.

I really began to see my drive to go to school for what it was: selfishness. I wasn't waiting on God to open a door; I was trying to drive a bulldozer through the wall. I had heard of a scriptural principle called "Death of a Vision" wherein God gives you an intense longing to do something for Him and then lets you try to achieve it under your own strength until you give up. Only then can He fulfill that desire in His way and in His time.

At the time I worked for a phone company. One day, driving to another service call in my truck, I pulled to the side of the road and bowed my head. I confessed that I had been acting selfishly, trying to do what I thought God wanted me to do. I acknowledged that I had been hurting Audrey by ignoring the closed doors. I would not try to force them open any longer. If He wanted me in school He would have to bring it about. Scripture teaches that God opposes the proud but gives grace to the humble. I was tired of being the former and desperately needed to become the latter.

I went home that evening and apologized to my wife, telling her that I would not bring up the subject again. She accepted my request for forgiveness. Then I told my pastor and his wife what I had prayed; both agreed that this had been the right thing to do.

What none of us could foresee was that less than two weeks later God would release an avalanche of provision and direction to make that very dream come true.

In a manner of speaking, the decision to let go of the drive to go to Bible school was a relief. It wasn't that I didn't still have the desire—it was that now it didn't *have me*. It was a question of control.

Although I didn't fully understand it at the time, this was the outworking of the principle in Genesis 4:7: "If you do not do well, sin is crouching at the door. Its desire is for you, but you must rule over it." Sin in the story underlying this verse was waiting for an opportunity to control Cain like a predator waiting at a door for a victim to devour. God was warning Cain that he had to master that urge.

The goal was good in my life, but the means was not. The relief came because the tension between Audrey and me disappeared. The inner tension was gone because the "peace of God, which surpasses all understanding, will guard your hearts and minds in Christ Jesus" (Philippians 4:7). His peace had replaced the sense that I had to work out the dream at all costs. I was still willing to go to school, but only if God would clearly open the door for both myself and my wife. I honestly had no hope of that happening at that point. I just trusted that God would work out His will in the matter.

I had gotten to that peace by obeying the admonition of Philippians 4:5-6: "Let your reasonableness be known to everyone. The Lord is at hand; do not be anxious about anything, but in everything by prayer and supplication with thanksgiving let your requests be made known to God." The Greek word translated as "reasonableness" is *epieikes*, a compound term that roughly means to fit upon— the idea of conforming gently, like a glove.

My previous approach had been anything but reasonable. Before I'd had strife; now I had peace. I liked the trade-in option. The Lord was at hand, and I had placed the matter in His hands.

Being out in my own work truck gave me the flexibility to stop home for lunch once in a while. About ten days after I submitted the issue of school to the Lord I came home at noon to find my wife sitting at the kitchen table with a somewhat concerned expression on her face.

"What's wrong?" I asked.

"I got a call from my mom," Audrey said. "She just got a letter from my Aunt Audrey out West. She received a large insurance payment after the death of her husband. She wrote to Mom to say she remembered hearing that you wanted to go to Bible school to become a pastor. Aunt Audrey said that if you still want to go she would be willing to help us financially."

You would think I would have been ecstatic. At that point, given my decision to drop the plan, I was more cautious and curious than anything else, not wanting to callously poke the wound Audrey had been dealing with because of my insistence on going to school.

"What does she mean by 'help us financially'?" I asked.

"I don't know; you'll have to call her," came the response. I could tell my wife was tense and confused.

I placed the call, and after chatting with Aunt Audrey for a few moments I asked her, "Mom told us you wrote. What do you mean by 'help us financially' to go to school?"

Long story short, she said, "If you will go to school to be a pastor I will give you eighteen thousand dollars, six thousand per year for three years to go."

As surprised as I was by her statement, I was concerned about how Audrey would react. After I got off the phone I was more stunned by my wife's reaction when I told her what Aunt Audrey had said.

"That's the hand of the Lord. It's time to go," came the matter-of-fact response.

Now I could be ecstatic.

My wife had been waiting for God to indicate His will without any manipulation on my part. This was what she needed for that confirmation. I felt as though I would explode with joy.

I didn't waste any time responding. We accepted Aunt Audrey's offer. It wouldn't cover all our expenses; with a wife and two little children I would still have to work part time. But it was a huge start. I went in to work that week, early in February of 1984, and turned in my resignation at the phone company, to be effective in August.

I have hated roller coasters my whole life. I had no idea the roller-coaster experience was exactly what the Christian life could feel like: sit down, shut up, and hang on!

The first bridge was burning, but I—or, more correctly, we—had no intention of turning back.

CHAPTER 7

Not Knowing

"And [Abraham] went out, not knowing where he was going."
Hebrews 11:8

I applied to and was accepted at Grand Rapids School of the Bible and Music, about 45 miles from our home. We went up to visit the school and look for housing options. GRSBM had married student housing, but it was all taken, with a long waiting list. Nothing else was available nearby. We started looking at housing possibilities farther away from the campus, but I was discouraged. I had really been looking forward to living close to campus to participate in campus life and married student fellowship events.

Still, it was only February, and there was plenty of time for something to work out. I really had a peace about trusting God after the call from Aunt Audrey. Resting in the peace that surpasses understanding (Philippians 4:7) was probably the most important lesson we learned through those days. It's peace that doesn't make sense from a purely human perspective.

The peace remained from February through April, though I wondered whether the lack of housing was an indication that we should just plan to remain in our home and I should commute. It would be a long daily drive, especially in Michigan winters. But if that was what it would take, there were some advantages to the idea.

We had purchased a house with 15 wooded acres, along with a small barn and pasture for Audrey's horse. A true fixer-upper, we had put a lot of labor and cash into it to make it livable. We had gotten it on a temporary land contract while we made improvements to the property, after which we sought FHA financing through a local savings and loan to pay off the land contract. Twice we applied, and twice we were given a list of things that needed to be done before approval of a loan. I accepted them in stride and went to work.

But the third time I went in for approval I got a third list.

"Wait a minute," I objected. "We completed the first list, and then I got a second list of new items. I completed all of those. These things were not on either of those lists. What's going on?"

The loan officer looked across the table sympathetically and simply said, "Steve, they don't want to give you the money." And that was the end of FHA financing as an option.

When Audrey's mom heard that we had been turned down, she offered to buy the land contract. We could pay her back, which would lower our payments and still provide a good return on her money. We accepted her offer.

Our piece of property had lots of oak trees to cut for firewood. With low payments and low heating costs we thought that, though remaining in our home rather than moving might be a financially tight option, we could make it work even if I were driving to school five days a week. This would mean giving up nearly all the campus life opportunities, but I was willing to let them go if I had to. I continued to have peace about it . . . until early May.

The peace left me one day like someone rolling up a window shade. I was mowing the yard when it happened. I stopped where I was, with the mower running and people driving by on the road. I knew I needed to pray about the situation right away.

"Lord, I have had peace up to this moment about all of this. But now I need you to show me what to do. If we are supposed to live here I have to get wood in soon so it can dry out for fall and winter.

If we are supposed to move I need to sell the truck I use to haul wood, and we will have to sell our house. You know I would love to live by the campus. Whatever you want is fine, but I need to know now." The peace came back just as immediately as it had left, and I went back to pushing my lawn mower. I told no one what I had prayed, not even Audrey.

Three days later a guy I had never met before pulled up into my driveway and rolled down his window. "I understand there's a truck for sale on this road," he told me. "Do you know where I can find it?"

There were no trucks for sale on my road. We lived on the edge of the Allegan State Forest, where there were few houses. I hadn't said anything to anyone about selling my truck. There was no "For Sale" sign on it. It wasn't even out by the road; it was out behind our barn. My head started spinning, and, at first, I didn't know what to say. Was this God answering my prayer? Or was it a fluke?

"I don't know of any trucks for sale on this road," I said, feeling as though I were dreaming. "I have been thinking about selling mine but really hadn't made up my mind." I was lying. Selling the truck had been an option for months, but I was honestly so astonished that this was happening that I couldn't think of how else to respond. I was still uncomfortable telling people that God was that involved in the details of my life and that the person in front of me had come as an answer to prayer.

"Let me take a look," and with that he got out of his car. "I just wrecked my truck and am looking for a replacement. As we rounded the corner of the barn, he exclaimed, "This is exactly what I'm looking for! How much do you want?" He was as shocked as I was.

I hadn't even started the truck up at that point. It ran fine, but there were no rear brake parts, and it needed a universal joint in the front end. The previous owner hadn't told me about those minor details when I bought it. At that moment I wondered if I needed to tell this potential buyer.

But those two verses came to mind: "Trust in the LORD with all your heart, and do not lean on your own understanding. In all your ways acknowledge him, and he will make straight your paths" (Proverbs 3:5-6). I knew the Lord wanted me to tell the guy about the brakes and u-joint, so I did.

"That's no problem—I'm a mechanic. How much do you want?" he insisted. I named a price, he made an offer, and I countered it. He gave me cash, came back the next day, and took the truck. Suddenly I had no means for hauling firewood, no way to stay in our present home without it, and no job after August.

But I had the peace that surpasses understanding, and it would last until the middle of June.

I could say we spent the next few weeks making plans to move in August. But that would be false. There were no plans that could be made. We didn't know from one day to the next what was going to happen. I can't even say the reality of how God would direct us based on my life verse had sunk in. He was indeed showing us one step at a time . . . and no more. In retrospect, I would have to say that we didn't realize it was happening—it just was. I can truthfully say we were pretty much along for the ride.

We knew that without the truck to haul firewood we were committed to selling the house, but we didn't have a clue where to start. We had never before sold a house, and for that matter we had only just bought ours in a far from normal fashion. The housing market was depressed in 1984 because the economy was experiencing a downturn. Houses could sit unsold for months, or even years. We had tried three times unsuccessfully to get conventional financing for the very property we were hoping to sell.

To complicate the situation, we had put a lot of repair money into the house and barn. New roofs on both, a new well, gutting the house to insulate and rewire—it all added up to far more than we could expect to get back. I was afraid that if we tried to sell it through a realtor we would lose all of that to the commission. We started praying on and off for wisdom about what to do, but none seemed to come.

One day my wife and I were sitting at the kitchen table pondering what that next step might be when a thought occurred to me. "You know," I said to Audrey, "Scripture teaches that God owns the whole planet. Why don't we ask him if He wants to sell a piece of it?" I know how that must have sounded. We thought it was crazy too, but we were slowly getting used to crazy. It was to become a lifestyle in more ways than we realized at the time.

I bowed my head and acknowledged God's ownership of the world. "We know we need to sell the house, but we don't know if we should go to a realtor or not, and we're running out of time."

At this point I want to add a word of caution about time crunches. Israel's first king, Saul, was a man handpicked by God for the role. Even so, Yahweh would eventually express displeasure over putting him in charge and actually remove him from that role, instead making David king.

Although Saul had some impressive qualities to go with his good looks, he also had a weakness that undermined his leadership. He was impulsive under pressure and consequently acted without asking God for wisdom. He simply assumed he knew the right thing to do in his circumstances. He might have thought that all he needed to do was take action and that God would sort out the details later. But that is not a good approach to following God.

Based on the circumstances that had unfolded already, it was clear that the house would have to be sold. But I wanted to make sure that I was not ignoring God's will and purpose.

My prayer was simple but direct. Even at that I didn't feel as though I were telling God what to do. "I'm going to run a plain classified ad in our paper for one week. If you want to sell it that way, great; otherwise, we will know we need to list it with a realtor." I don't know which was crazier, asking God to sell our house or believing that a realtor could do it within a couple of weeks in the prevailing housing market.

We ran the bare bones classified with one prominent feature, the price. We had bought the place for about $25,000. Now, you can surmise it wasn't something out of *Better Homes and Gardens*—more like a woodshed out of *BHaG*. But lots of cash and paint had gone a long way. We decided to price it at $35,000.

We got a couple of inquiries, but nothing solid. It was starting to look as though we would have to list with a realtor when we got a call from a guy and his fiancée who wanted to come look at it.

We walked them through barn and house with them making mental notes, ending up back in the kitchen where Audrey and I had prayed. Then he popped the question: "How much would you take for it?"

The only way I know to describe what happened next is to say that time slowed down, as in those silly scenes on TV where someone is thinking while other stuff is going on around him in slow motion. But my brain went into high gear as the thoughts poured through it.

I had put the price we felt we needed in the paper—one that would pay off the property and still give us something to help with living expenses at school. We didn't feel it was unreasonable, given how much we had invested in cash and sweat equity. But if I insisted on the asking price he might respond that he would think about it and call us. We might not hear from them again.

In my heart I shot up a panic prayer. "What do I say, Lord?" Immediately Proverbs 3:5–6 came back to mind, but this time part of it was like a 90-point font: "IN ALL YOUR WAYS ACKNOWLEDGE HIM, AND HE WILL MAKE STRAIGHT YOUR PATHS." I got the point. The Lord wanted me to tell the guy why I was selling the house. I had to stop hiding the truth that we were seeking and following God's will for our lives.

"To be honest, I quit my job and am selling the house to go to

Bible school to become a pastor," I said. "I need to ask $35,000." I have never forgotten his response.

"Okay, I'll go to the bank and get the money."

It was that simple—no dickering back and forth. He went to the same savings and loan we had gone to, applied for the same FHA financing we had been turned down for three times, and got it without any questions. They never even conducted another inspection of the property. The buyer took care of everything involved in selling the home, even expenses the seller would normally incur and all the legal work. All we had to do was sign our names.

So now I would have no job as of August, along with no truck and no house. Yet we still had nowhere to move to and no income to supplement the money from Aunt Audrey. But there was one thing I did have: the peace that surpasses understanding came back . . . this time until early August.

We were at a big church potluck dinner at Merson Church when the peace disappeared. We were finished eating, and I was about to walk upstairs from the basement when it happened. By now I had gotten the picture. When the peace left it was time to pray. So I stopped to pray . . . right there in the middle of the stairway. I acknowledged the Lord's direction and provision up to that point and reminded Him of our submission to His will. "We have nowhere to live, and I need a job. Whatever you want is fine with me—you just need to show me."

The peace came rushing back, and I walked from the bottom to the top of the stairs in the lobby. At that moment our pastor's wife, Joan Pike, walked out of his office and asked, "Steve, did Shari tell you about the house in Grand Rapids?" Their daughter worked at the school I was going to attend.

"No," I responded.

"Her supervisor just bought a house across the street from the campus. He wants to convert it into a duplex, and she was telling him about you. She is pretty sure he would hire you to do the work, and you could get the lower apartment."

The hair stood up on the back of my neck as it sank in that it hadn't taken 45 seconds for the Lord to answer my prayer for both a home and a job. The house, at 1313 Thomas, turned out to be perfect, right across the street from the building where most of my classes were to meet.

I got the job to remodel the house into a duplex, and we got the lower apartment. Shari and another girl from our home church, Rinda, moved into the upper unit. The owner of the house let Audrey pick carpeting, paint, and even flooring and cabinets for our kitchen. It was a huge encouragement to her to see God give this provision to meet not only my needs and desires but hers as well.

"[Abraham] went out, not knowing where he was going . . ." (Hebrews 11:8). It was almost mind-boggling. A few short months earlier I had clearly come to the realization that God would not allow me to make long-range plans for my life and then work them out under my own steam and from my own resources. The whole process had been out of my control. And yet it hadn't been . . .

We had simply believed, accepted, and responded to promises. It had been necessary for us to act on them, and then wait for the next door to appear. And now it was not just me who was obeying God's calling. God had called my wife too, just as Pastor Pike had said he would.

The journey had begun, and now we were taking the steps together instead of me dragging my wife behind me. That was to be crucial, because as hard as school would be, an event was coming that would threaten to derail everything.

God is able to do far more abundantly than we could ever think or ask. Sometimes we do not have because we do not ask, or we ask with wrong motives, wanting to fee our selfish desires (James 4:2–3).

"I waited patiently for the LORD;
    he inclined to me and heard my cry." Psalm 40:1

Little did we know then that we would do a lot of crying to the Lord in the days to come.

CHAPTER 8

Disaster and Deliverance

I was standing in a hospital room doorway watching the Challenger spacecraft liftoff from the Kennedy Space Center in Houston. The tenth launch of a shuttle orbiter, it had all become so routine that many people did not even watch launches anymore. I really needed to get back to my Bible school classes, but the launches still fascinated me, so I stood in the doorway to watch for a moment before leaving St. Mary's Hospital in Grand Rapids for school.

Suddenly, the world watched with me as an event in real time changed our concept of the safety of space travel. One of the solid rocket booster seals breached, and subsequently the main fuel tank exploded abruptly, ending the flight—and the lives of all seven crew members. Disaster gripped our hearts and attention in the middle of what should have been a routine flight.

But I was in the hospital in the middle of a disaster of my own, one that threatened to end the dream that had lifted off only a few months earlier in my life. My circumstances were not as tragic as what I had just witnessed, but I did not see how my own situation could look much bleaker than it currently did.

In the fall of 1985 I was carrying a full 16 credit hours at Grand Rapids School of the Bible and Music, doing all the associated course work in my "spare time" outside the classroom. I was also working twenty hours per week and still trying to spend as much time as I could with my wife and two daughters, five-year-old Jen and three-year-old Kris.

The previous summer had turned into an unexpected ministry opportunity. We had been invited to join the summer staff of Camp Barakel in northern Michigan. I would work as an activities programmer and chapel leader. My hours usually ran from 7 a.m. to 11 p.m.—long for both myself and my wife, who basically had to watch the kids all day every day with no real house of our own to turn them loose in.

To help keep up her sanity and health, she had decided to start jogging when I or someone else could watch the girls. Nothing aggressive, but enough to help her stay active.

But on one of those routine runs in the woods she felt a pain in her lower back, and it didn't go away. When we moved back home in August she got chiropractic adjustments for several weeks, but the situation only got worse—a lot worse.

By December she was in so much pain that I literally had to ask one of my classmates to help me carry her to our station wagon and lay her in "the way back" of the car. We drove her to a neurosurgeon for evaluation, carrying her (in tears) into the doctor's office, much to the shock of those in the waiting room. That was when my dream started to turn into a nightmare.

When we had lived in the work world, my health insurance had covered her. But when we went to Bible school we faced the dilemma of what to use to replace that umbrella. As a student I had basic coverage through the school, but we could not afford independent insurance for Audrey and the girls. After much prayer and consideration, we decided we would have to trust the Lord for them. We had no idea how much trust that was going to entail.

The doctor diagnosed her with at least one severely ruptured disk in the lumbar section at the base of her spine. She would need surgery. When the doctor learned I was in Bible school, he offered to do the surgery at a reduced price, and the hospital had some grant money for those without insurance. Still, the ultimate out-of-pocket cost for getting my wife back to health was going to be substantial, and I eventually realized that the impact of the injury would affect more than just my wife's mobility and ability to fully function as a mom for the girls.

At the very least, I would have to drastically reduce my hours at school to care for my family and at the same time be able to work more hours to cover the costs. But the catch was that the money Aunt Audrey was supplying for school depended on my maintaining a fulltime student status. That was impossible under our current situation. After talking to Aunt Audrey, we learned that she was willing to indefinitely suspend the payments she was sending us until I could return to fulltime status.

This was a double whammy. Not only would I need to work more hours, but we would lose the funding for school that we had been receiving every month.

I was about as discouraged as I could get. All I had wanted since I received Jesus as my Savior was the opportunity to go to school and be equipped for ministry. I loved preaching and teaching the Bible. But my love and responsibility for my family had to take priority. Reducing my class load to the minimum of 12 credit hours for fulltime status would still not allow me to add enough work hours to meet the financial need—not to mention the homework outside the classroom—while also trying to be more available to Audrey and the girls.

But I would slowly come to realize that my discouragement had a deeper foundation, one I did not like to grasp. I was discouraged in part because of my pride.

I had wanted to go to Bible school and graduate with straight As. My motivation didn't stem from a pure desire to simply do everything well for the Lord's sake. It went back further to a longing to negate a history of poor performance all my previous life as a student. With undiagnosed ADD symptoms, Bs had often been the best I could do, with Cs and Ds all too common on my report cards.

Now I would see them again, with relation to far more important studies. The old shame came back to haunt me as I realized I would be lucky to pass my classes at all. It was better in my mind to give up on school than to go through that. What I didn't realize at that moment was that God wasn't going to let me dodge that bullet. He wanted me healed as much as He did my wife, and that meant dealing with a ruptured disk in my pride.

Reluctantly, I called Pastor Pike back at Merson Church on a Sunday afternoon, to let him know I would have to drop out of school for the foreseeable future so I could start working full-time. He listened as I laid out the situation for him, and I think it genuinely troubled him. GRSBM was his alma mater, and he had been the first one to have seen that God had given me raw gifts for preaching and teaching that had to be refined. But while he had empathy for me, he didn't have a solution. He let me know that he and the church would be praying for me.

Just as when I'd had to let go of school in the first place, I had to do so once again. In some ways it was harder to relinquish something I already had. Before this had entailed only letting go of a dream—now it was letting go of reality.

One of the most important lessons in the Christian life is to learn to hold the things God entrusts to you with open hands, not clenched fists. How many become "nones" precisely because they think God has failed them? As soon as we seize resources, positions of responsibility, or spiritual giftings and wrap our lives around them, ownership changes. Our hearts and attitudes cause us to stop being stewards of the kingdom. As I hung up the phone I acknowledged that ownership belonged to the Lord. In Job's words, "The LORD gave, and the LORD has taken away; blessed be the name of the LORD" (Job 1:21).

But a short time after I hung up, the phone rang. It was Pastor Pike. He wanted to know how much financial help we would require to stay in school. I had absolutely no idea. He wondered whether there were people in our congregation who could help us for a few months. He would ask for an informal show of hands at the evening service. He asked whether $1,500 a month would get us by for the semester until I could work fulltime in the summer. Once again, I had no clue how much the medical bills would be, but that sounded like a reasonable figure. He said he would get back to me after the evening service and hung up. I believe that "for those who love God all things [even hard things] work together for good, for those who are called according to his purpose" (Romans 8:28), but I was experiencing emotional whiplash.

Pastor Pike called back later that evening; he said that he felt the members of the church would be able to supply $1,500 a month and asked whether I could commit to staying in school. We were overwhelmed by the generosity of the congregation, and I said that I would. In reality, Merson Church never once gave us $1,500 a month. They always exceeded their financial commitment to us, sometimes by a significant amount.

I went back to school and reduced my credit hours to the minimum number to retain fulltime status. I would make up the required credits by correspondence courses during the summer. The hardest part for me was going to my instructors to ask what the minimum requirements would be to pass their classes. My pride had to be sacrificed in the face of those I wanted to please and impress. I would do the required reading, take the best notes I could in class, and just hope I didn't fail any of the quizzes or tests. My grades that semester were not what I would have wanted, but they were good enough for me to pass all of my courses.

Audrey's surgery had taken place in the early morning just before the Challenger exploded. The surgeon came to me in the waiting area and reported that the surgery had been successful but that it had been the worst rupture he had ever worked on. The nerve had suffered so much trauma that she would have some numbness in the side of her leg and foot that would never leave.

Merson Church completely trusted us and never asked us to supply the bills we were receiving as proof of our stewardship. So I didn't keep track of running totals. As bills came in we paid them.

But at the end of the year, when tax time came, I had to round up all our bills from the surgery and add up the check amounts from the gifts we received. As I did so I could hardly believe what was coming to light on paper.

After itemizing all the bills from the hospital and doctor, and adding the amounts of the checks from Merson, we were astonished to find that our home church had given us exactly what we needed to pay all of the out-of-pocket expenses without our ever telling them how much we owed. We finished the semester without any surgery-based debt.

Jesus said, "Seek first the kingdom of God and his righteousness, and all these things will be added to you" (Matthew 6:33). Those things were indeed "added" to us through the kindness of our brothers and sisters in Christ as they were led by the Holy Spirit— no more and no less than what we needed.

That was one of the most dramatic specific provisions of the Lord to meet our needs, but this instance was far from the only time we saw Him give us exactly what we needed precisely when we needed it.

CHAPTER 9

The Tax Man Cometh

When we joined the staff of Camp Barakel we had only about $300 per month of pledged support, not even close to what we needed. The camp would provide housing and some basic food supplies from the kitchen, but we were responsible for electricity and phone service. Our budget was extremely tight. No, our budget was *a joke*.

At the time we had the choice to opt in or out of Social Security as Christian missionaries. But we were still responsible for self-employment income taxes because all of us on staff were there as volunteers. We needed to make quarterly payments to keep up.

In the Gospel of Matthew an interesting story is recorded in chapter 17, where Jesus and Matthew are responsible to pay tax.

"When they came to Capernaum, the collectors of the two-drachma tax went up to Peter and said, 'Does your teacher not pay the tax?' He said, 'Yes.' And when he came into the house, Jesus spoke to him first, saying, 'What do you think, Simon? From whom do kings of the earth take toll or tax? From their sons or from others?' And when he said, 'From others,' Jesus said to him, 'Then the sons are free. However, not to give offense to them, go to the sea and cast a hook and take the first fish that comes up, and when you open its mouth you will find a shekel.

Take that and give it to them for me and for yourself.'" Matthew
17:24–27

I would love to be able to tell a story of catching a fish and finding the exact amount in its mouth to pay our quarterly payment of
$200. Unfortunately, there were no fish in the camp lake capable of
carrying that much change and still swimming. Even if there had
been, I would have needed a trawler to pull one up.

The apostle Paul taught that Christians are responsible to pay
"taxes to whom taxes are owed" (Romans 13:7). But what do you
do when the payment comes due and you simply do not have the
money? I remembered not just the stories in Scripture but the times
we had already seen the Lord provide to meet our needs.

I gathered our little family in the kitchen of our house (I am not
sure why so many of our prayers took place in the kitchen), and we
sought the Lord together.

I acknowledged God's calling and leading in our lives, and our
responsibility to pay taxes. We had no money in the bank for the
payment, and I refused to let people know we needed help with it.
We simply asked God to do what He had promised to do.

The next day, in the mail, was a letter from some close friends
from our days at Merson Church, Marv and Gretta Veldhoff. We
had really enjoyed their fellowship prior to going to Bible school
but had not been able to maintain close contact with them since we
had moved more than two hundred miles away to the north woods.

They had read our previous month's prayer letter we had sent
to the church, which said nothing of our tax need. But they felt the
Lord would have them send us a gift. In the envelope was a check
for exactly $200.

One of the most important aspects of praying that brings God
glory is learning to pray for exactly what we need. The fruit of that
principle came up over and over again in our lives.

I remember a time when we wanted our oldest daughter to attend a seminar, but the registration fee was $75—that we did not have. I took my daughter aside and prayed with her that the Lord would provide either the $75 or the means to get it so she could attend. I specifically asked the Lord to provide the exact amount so we would know that was what we were to spend it on, since there were lots of other needs for extra money.

Within a week or so Jennifer came home excited. "Guess what! I got a job!" she exclaimed. It was difficult for staff kids to earn any money living out in the countryside with few neighbors nearby. "Great!" I said, "Doing what?" "Raking leaves," she replied, apparently unaware of how much work that might entail with us living in an area covered by huge oak trees. But I didn't want to be the one to break the news and dampen her enthusiasm.

Still, maybe it would be worth her while, especially with so few options available. "How much will you be paid?"

"Seventy-five dollars!" she said, obviously already envisioning what she would spend it on.

Suddenly I remembered my prayer. I looked at her. "Jen, do you remember what we prayed?"

Her face fell.

"Jen, we prayed that the Lord would provide exactly $75 or the means to get it, so we would know that He meant for it to pay the seminar fee. We need to send it in for that."

"I know," she said—"I remember"—now looking at the floor. I felt terrible to shoot down her desires. It was so rare for our kids to have money of their own based on their own efforts.

"We need to send in that money for the seminar, but I promise to find a way to pay it all back to you." It was the best I could do as her dad. She raked the very large yard, and we sent the money off.

A couple of weeks earlier I had asked our Sunday school class to pray with us for God to provide the funds we needed for Jen to attend the seminar. One of the elderly ladies came to me after we had sent in the fee and said she wanted to provide the money. I would have felt terrible taking it from her when so many retirees have a difficult time making ends meet. So I was relieved to be able to tell her the money had already been provided, while thanking her for her generous offer.

Surprised, she looked at me for a moment. Then she insisted, "No, I am supposed to give this to you." She would not take no for an answer, handing me $75.

I was so thrilled when I went back to Jen and gave her the money. "You honored God by putting His will first with the money we sent away. Now He has rewarded your faith by returning the money to you."

There were so many other stories like this in our journey, but you might wonder why the Lord hadn't simply supplied more monthly support. The truth is that I have found it to be a pattern in my life that when I have resources available my faith in the Lord to provide diminishes.

I would not trade what we have seen Him do for what we might have wished we had in hand.

CHAPTER 10

Beyond Our Limitations

"You do not have, because you do not ask." James 4:2

One of my great failings in my walk with the Lord has been my tendency to rely on my own abilities and neglect to ask for help at the start of a project or task. That isn't always the case, but I must admit that it happens far too often.

One of the most important aspects of being a disciple of Jesus is making what you have available to meet the needs of others. The whole nature of spiritual gifting revolves around Christians being equipped by the Holy Spirit to minister to others. Sometimes that takes on a supernatural dimension, while in other cases it is simply a natural thing, such as giving food, drink, or clothing to those less fortunate than ourselves.

But confusion can come about by separating supernatural and natural ministry. They are not mutually exclusive, and all too often I have discovered that I have been ministering in the flesh when God wanted, or in some cases needed, to be more directly involved.

I had worked for many years as a telephone installer and repairman, and had studied digital electronics, so it was a natural fit for me to become the de facto phone technician at the Christian camp where we served.

But trusting exclusively on my training and experience often meant that I would work fruitlessly for hours on a difficult problem in our phone system after a thunderstorm, often late into the night or early morning. My wife would call my phone room and ask when I would be coming home, to which the answer would usually be, "I don't know. I can't find the problem."

The question that inevitably followed was, "Have you prayed and asked for help?"

To which I would always sheepishly respond, "No, not yet." I don't know why the question grated on me, but it might have been a matter of pride. I couldn't estimate the number of times I would get off the phone, pray, and within five minutes would have found and fixed the problem.

For many years I enjoyed snorkel diving. I had always been fascinated by the underwater world and could hold my breath for nearly two minutes. As a result, it wasn't uncommon for people to ask me to find things that had been dropped in the camp lake. Sometimes this was easy, but other times the soft, mucky bottom sucked such items up pretty quickly.

One day a summer camp staffer came to me and reported that a camper had lost his glasses off the edge of the dock at the waterfront. The staffer gave me a pretty specific location near one of the ladders, an area that wasn't weedy, so I figured I could find them fairly easily after everyone else had gone up to supper. The trick would be not stirring up the silt while I was searching, but I had already set myself up to fail.

I pulled on my mask and fins and jumped in. It was a gorgeous afternoon, and the lake was the perfect temperature for a swim after a long, hard day of work cutting firewood.

In order to not stir up the bottom, I decided I would have to search nearly inverted, with head down and feet up, to make sure my fins didn't stir up the silt. The water was surprisingly clear after a day of campers being at the waterfront. The sun was still high, so all things considered I should be done quickly, leaving plenty of time for me to prepare for evening Bible study.

I gave myself a search area of about a hundred square feet in case the glasses had drifted at an angle. I slowly swam with my facemask about six inches off the bottom without touching the silt. I methodically crisscrossed the search area, moving over a foot or two and swimming back. The awkward swim position was challenging, especially because I couldn't kick and come up quickly for air. After several unfruitful attempts at covering the area, and even expanding it to two hundred square feet, I decided I had to change strategy.

Now as I swam I slowly ran my fingertips through the silt as I crisscrossed. No luck. I searched under the dock. Nothing. I could hardly believe it. I was running out of time because I was losing light, I had evening responsibilities, and now the bottom was getting more stirred up with every trip down.

I started moving more quickly across the search area on each pass, running my hands side to side an inch or two into the muck. I couldn't even see the bottom now and was proceeding completely by feel. But to no avail. I finally ran out of time and energy. The only thing I could think was that someone searching earlier, perhaps without a mask, had pushed the glasses deeper into the muck.

I came up by the edge of the dock where the staffer had indicated the glasses had gone in, but this time, beyond just taking a breath, I prayed. As best I can remember I prayed, "Lord, I am out of time. Please help me find these glasses for the camper. I am going down one more time to stick my hand in the muck. If it would please you, let me put my hand right on the glasses." I took a breath and headed quickly to the bottom I couldn't see and stuck my hand straight down about six inches into the muck.

And there they were.

I have found it a fairly consistent principle in my life that when I am depending on my own abilities the Lord lets me go until I come to the end of myself. Would I have found the glasses instantly if I had prayed the same thing the first time I got into the water? I don't know. Did the Lord want me to recognize that all my skill and effort were not the answer to the need? I think so. All I know for certain is that there was nothing more I could have done but ask for help. And I got it immediately.

Paul taught that when we are weak, then we are strong (2 Corinthians 12:10). God loves to take us to the end of our limitations.

It is only then that it becomes clear that it was God who was at work, even if that working was accomplished through us as His instrument of choice.

CHAPTER 11

Truth in Love

Without question, one of the most difficult aspects of being a minister is confronting sin. This is doubly difficult when you believe the person does not know the Lord, yet thinks he or she is a Christian.

The apostle Paul wrote of the need to "carefront," as a friend of mine, Roger Williams, once put it:

> "Rather, speaking the truth in love, we are to grow up in every way into him who is the head, into Christ, from whom the whole body, joined and held together by every joint with which it is equipped, when each part is working properly, makes the body grow so that it builds itself up in love." Ephesians 4:15-16

If done incorrectly, this approach can foster anger and resentment. Sometimes, when the person is not willing to receive the admonition, that will happen even if it is given gently. But if the Holy Spirit guides our words, our heart for the person is sincere, and the seeds of truth are allowed to take root, the effect can be profound in a person's life.

His name was John. He was a terrific kid, a hard worker, fun to have on the crew. I really liked having him. But something troubled me about him.

For all the positives I could see about him, I could tell something was wrong. In Bible studies he could give all the right responses. He was the typical youth group kid, having grown up in a Bible church setting with Christian parents. But I could sense that this was a mask he would wear around Christian leaders. He could make the right noises, but I could see that his heart was not in it, and that put me in a tight spot.

The author of the book of Hebrews wrote, "Obey your leaders and submit to them, for they are keeping watch over your souls, as those who will have to give an account. Let them do this with joy and not with groaning, for that would be of no advantage to you" (Hebrews 13:17).

A watchman was someone who stood guard on the city wall, or in a tower, and called out if he saw an enemy approaching so that those who depended on him could take shelter, or take up swords for conflict. This was a great responsibility, and the lives of many might depend on one or two taking it seriously. I knew I was a watchman in John's life, and I needed to warn him about what I saw. I prayed that the Lord would guide my words, give me a heart of compassion, and open a door of ministry to him.

One evening after the wood crew had finished another day of labor in the woods gathering firewood for camp, I invited him to the game room for some ping-pong and bumper pool. We were both very competitive, and it was just plain fun to spend time together.

After a half hour or so, I asked him to sit down so we could talk. I expressed my appreciation for his hard work and told him how much I enjoyed having him on the crew. But eventually I moved to sharing my concern over where his heart was in relationship to the Lord. To the best of my ability I spoke the "truth in love" (Ephesians 4:15), and I made every effort to make it clear that I was not condemning him but leaving open the possibility that I might be misguided in my observations.

As I spoke John just hung his head. No anger or resentment

boiled up. He just looked at the floor. But I finally reached the point where I had to gently say, "John, I hate to say it, but I have to tell you I don't see any proof that you really know Jesus as your Savior." No response.

Looking back, I can't even call it a conversation. The entire time John never said a word. By the time I was finished, the silence was deafening. I let him go back to the rest of the group, feeling as though I would probably never see him again after that week at camp. And for several years I didn't.

Then at a winter teen retreat a voice called out to me in the dining hall, "Steve, Steve! Do you remember me?" I looked up, surprised, as this tall, lanky guy came bounding through the tables and people.

It was John.

"Of course I do, John! It's so good to see you again. After that time in the game room when you didn't respond to me, I was afraid I had offended you and would never see you again."

"No," he said. "I knew you were right, and I didn't know what to say. But I got saved recently! I want to go into youth ministry." He was radiant, and I was full of joy for him. The light that had been missing from his eyes before was there now.

I hadn't decided before our initial confrontation that John wasn't saved, and I didn't tell him he wasn't. I just told him that I didn't see evidence that he was.

Enthusiasm is not proof of a genuine, saving relationship with Jesus. But lack of the joy that comes from knowing Jesus as Lord and Savior may be indicative that a person is just going through the motions. It was speaking the truth in love that opened the door for the Holy Spirit to bring conviction about what was missing.

CHAPTER 12

Pressed Down, Shaken Together

I walked up the path from my car toward the dilapidated old farm-house. I hadn't seen my friends, the Meads, for quite a while. But the Lord had spoken specifically to me about giving some money to them that my wife and I had been trying to squirrel away for ourselves. Even so, I was excited to see them again, and to bless them with the money, even though it was not a huge amount.

As I handed them the cash and explained that the Lord had asked me to give it to them, they looked at it like it was radioactive. "What's wrong?" I asked. They were genuinely as surprised to receive the money as I had been for God to ask me to give it away. But I should not have been surprised at the divine request.

The temptation for any of us when we have little is to try to hang on to it. The nice way to refer to that mentality is to dress it up and categorize it as a survival instinct. But we need to call it what it is: fear. It is the fear that our wellbeing is totally in our own hands, leaving God and His provision out of the picture.

It is in giving in to fear that we deny God the opportunity to inject unexpected blessing and provision into our lives. Instead of being channels of blessing to others, we trust our own resources and cling to what we possess. Jesus taught His disciples exactly the opposite mentality as their guiding perspective.

It was in one of those moments in our lives when we ourselves had little that the Lord asked us to give away what we did have to a family in need. The Lord was about to take advantage of an opportunity to show us what a "good measure, pressed down, shaken together, running over" (Luke 6:28) looks like when He pours it into our lap.

While I was pastoring there was no extra money for anything, let alone a vacation. Audrey and I hadn't been able to do anything fun on our own for a long time. But one day we decided we had to make this a priority and started scraping together a few dollars here and there to save toward the opportunity for some time away.

It was very slow going, but eventually we had about $75 saved. Barely even seed money, but it was a start. I was praying in our den one day when a home missionary family, Dave and Beulah Mead and their sons, came to my mind. They traveled around Michigan as a family doing music ministry in churches and camps. I really had come to love and appreciate them but hadn't seen them in a while. As I prayed for them I came to the realization that God wanted me to give our money to them and trust Him for a vacation for ourselves.

They lived over 160 miles away in Gladwin, Michigan, but I needed, anyway, to make a trip north that would take me much closer to them. I decided to swing by and drop off the money unannounced to surprise them, rather than simply mailing it. I did not realize at the time how important hand delivery would be, or that I would be as surprised as they were.

I drove to their place, an old two-story that hadn't seen a new coat of paint in years. As I walked up to the house I was anticipating seeing them again and encouraging them with the gift. I wasn't, however, prepared for the greeting I got.

As the door opened, the entire family was there, dressed up, ready to go somewhere. They had the oddest looks on their faces as I handed them the money and explained that I felt God had asked me to give it to them. "What's wrong?" I asked.

"We have a ministry trip to go on and no money for gas. This is just what we need for the trip," came the reply. I was blown away.

I was ecstatic after I left their house at what had happened when I obeyed the very specific prompting of the Lord. I had been directed to this family at the very moment they needed help. My trust would now be in the Lord to meet our need.

Jesus said, "Give, and it will be given to you. Good measure, pressed down, shaken together, running over, will be put into your lap. For with the measure you use it will be measured back to you" (Luke 6:38). I was about to find out how big a measuring cup the Lord likes to use.

A week or so later our friends Gary and Dory called. They were both on the phone and excited. We didn't hear from or see them often enough because they lived in Florida when they weren't bicycling around the U.S. on evangelistic tours.

"We have been praying for you guys," they said, "and we believe God wants us to pay to fly you down to stay with us for a week in Miami. It won't cost you anything but what you want to spend out of pocket." We were stunned. They had absolutely no idea about our desire for a vacation or our giving our money to the Meads. It doesn't seem fair in comparison to consider this as a pressed down, shaken together version of the little we had given away.

Paul burst forth in praise over the provision, power, and direction of God: "Now to him who is able to do far more abundantly than all that we ask or think, according to the power at work within us, to him be glory in the church and in Christ Jesus throughout all generations, forever and ever. Amen" (Ephesians 3:20–21).

We never would have thought to ask for something that big, nor did we ask for it. We just responded when He asked for our "fishes and loaves" to meet someone else's needs while trusting Him for our own.

What we didn't realize in that moment of excitement is that the trip itself was about to require last-minute trust in the Lord's provision. Without it the trip still would not have happened, despite of the generous obedience of our friends.

CHAPTER 13

My, Oh My, Miami

A trip to Miami. We had to pinch ourselves—several times. It almost felt as though we had just dreamed it. But it was true, and we needed to quickly hammer out the details of time away from my responsibilities as a pastor and to farm out our four kids.

My secretary at the church, Jane, agreed to keep our two oldest for the time we were gone. Audrey's mom, Ann, would take the two youngest for the week. Pieces of the vacation puzzle quickly fell into place. Our friends paid for our airline tickets, and we were to take an early flight out of Kalamazoo on February 21, 1994, direct to Miami. We dropped off Jen and Kris with Jane in Port Huron, and Mom and her husband, Gerald, awaited us in Allegan to leave Sarah and Allison with them.

Allegan, the town where I had grown up, was two hundred miles away. The plan was to make the trip from Port Huron to Allegan the evening before we flew out, drop off Sarah and Allison, sleep there ourselves, and then make a quick trip to Kalamazoo in the morning for an early flight. Well, that was the plan, at least.

When we headed for Allegan, we had the van packed to the hilt. We needed to take everything necessary to keep the girls happy and occupied at Grandma's house for a week, and Audrey and I had several bags packed for our stay in Miami. The one thing conspicuously lacking was my toolbox. As a driver of old cars, I rarely take a long trip without my tools, just in case. But this time I did not put them in the van, and I was about to discover how big a mistake that was.

Traffic was good, and the weather, although cold, was not a problem. February was the perfect time to head for a week's stay with our friends in Miami. We got loaded up and left with enough time for the three-hour drive to Allegan. We would arrive late, but that would be fine. We were so excited we would probably not sleep much anyway. As it would turn out, I didn't sleep at all.

The trip across the Mitten, as Michigan is affectionately known, was uneventful until about halfway to Allegan. Driving down the expressway at night I suddenly noticed that the dashboard lights in the van seemed to be getting dim, and then I noticed that the headlights also seemed to be less bright. At first I was hoping this was my imagination, but as the seconds ticked by it became clear: we were losing the alternator in the van.

We were going to get off the I-69 expressway at Charlotte and head straight west to Allegan. But as we came up to the stop sign on the ramp I kept the van moving toward a gas station just to my right. The engine completely died just as we approached the lights of the canopy, and we rolled to a stop near the building. A quick look under the hood told me we were not going any farther. The bearings were shot in the alternator.

It was late enough that nothing was open for repairs. The night manager of the gas station gave me permission to push the van into a space on the side of the lot until morning. We contacted Audrey's mom and asked whether they could come to pick up our girls at the airport, which they agreed to do.

We bundled them up in their car seats as best we could for the night, and Audrey just sobbed. I tried to encourage her, but honestly, I did not see a way I could get us out of the situation we were in. Even if I could fix the van in the morning, we were still over an hour from the airport in Kalamazoo. I spent much time praying, asking the Lord what to do.

We all stayed in the van, and I tried to doze. The others slept, but for me that was impossible. The minutes dragged by like hours as I listened to Audrey and the girls breathing. I finally decided to go inside to sit in the station eating area. At least it was warm, and I could read newspapers and pray.

I have always tried to steer conversations with people toward an opportunity to share with them about the Lord. As I sat and read the paper while the night manager went about his duties, I started to wonder if this was a divine appointment. I began conversing with him, told him what we were doing, and basically shared my testimony with him.

It turned out he was a Christian, but because he worked nights he had been frustrated at his inability to have fellowship with other believers. We talked a lot about the things of the Lord that night. After all, we were both each other's captive audience.

During the course of conversation he told me there was an automotive parts store to the west about a mile. To the east was a Chrysler dealership about the same distance away. With little else to do I decided to walk to each of the businesses during the night to check on their posted hours of operation and determine what my best option would be to get an alternator as early as possible. The sky was totally clear and the wind completely calm. There wasn't a car on the highway as I trudged first to the parts store, then to the dealership, and back to the gas station to think out my plan.

Neither choice was good. The Chrysler dealership might be the best bet to have the alternator but opened for business far too late to leave enough time to make the airport. The parts store opened earlier but was less likely to have that particular alternator. Not only was I exhausted from lack of sleep, but the stress of trying to figure this out was draining my energy.

The time finally came to head out. I had decided to try the parts store first. I would walk there earlier than the advertised opening time, hoping that someone would arrive early and have pity on us. I walked to the counter in the gas station to thank the night manager for his information and conversation. He started quickly telling me he had been looking though the yellow pages to try to find a way to help me. He started rattling off other possibilities, and I started to get really annoyed.

I had spent all night trying to think through what to do, formulate a plan, and get ready to execute it. I knew the manager was just trying to be helpful, but I really had to get going as he turned the phonebook around and pushed it toward me. Aggggh!

I tried to pretend I was appreciative looking through what he was indicating as options, when I really wasn't even reading the listings. I just wanted to get out the door. Suddenly I had a sense that I needed to look at the page more closely. I noticed an obscure classified ad for a small automotive electrical shop in town, something the manager had not mentioned. I looked at the hours of operation—the shop would open before either the parts store or the dealership.

But there was a catch. A very small shop like this one generally does not have on hand a wide range of parts to pick from. As defective units come in they are usually repaired and picked back up. To make matters worse, I was used to having an oddball Chrysler minivan. The vehicle was an "American" brand, but the engine was a Mitsubishi. More than once I had run into having to wait on a parts store to order what I needed to work on it as a do-it-yourselfer. There was not enough time for the shop owner to rebuild my alternator. What were the odds they would have this alternator as a rebuilt on the shelf, ready to go? It was 7:00 a.m., the time the shop was to be open that day, so I called.

The answer was affirmative. Unbelievable. The gas station night manager offered to drive me there because the day manager had come onboard. He also got out his own tools for me to use. I worked as fast as I could to replace the alternator and jump the now dead battery.

When I finally got us headed for Kalamazoo, we had barely enough time to make the flight. If I had gone to either the parts store or the car dealership we would never have made our plane. But we did make it in time, handed over our two little girls to Grandma, and spent a wonderful week in Miami with our gracious friends.

It would be impossible to remember and recount all of the times we have seen the Lord intervene in meeting our financial needs as we have held fast to the promise, "Seek first the kingdom of God and his righteousness, and all these things will be added to you" (Matthew 6:33).

But some situations have been so remarkably precise in response to prayer that I will have to share them in some of the following chapters.

CHAPTER 14

Lost in Transmission

"Therefore do not be anxious, saying, 'What shall we eat?' or 'What shall we drink?' or 'What shall we wear?' For the Gentiles seek after all these things, and your heavenly Father knows that you need them all. But seek first the kingdom of God and his righteousness, and all these things will be added to you."
Matthew 6:31–33

After we had been on the camp staff for four and a half years we knew it was time for us to seek the Lord's timing to leave Christian camping. I had always wanted to seek pastoral ministry. One of the camp staff members asked me if we would be putting our names on lists of pastors looking for churches, to which I replied, "No."

Justifiably puzzled, he asked, "Well then, what will you do? How do you expect to find a church?"

"We'll just start saying goodbye to people we have known here at camp and let the Lord connect us with a church."

"I don't think that's how it works," he replied.

But that was indeed what we did, . . . and what God did. When someone we knew through camp heard we were leaving, she contacted the search committee for her church and asked them to contact me.

We spoke back and forth a couple of times, but as much as I wanted to pursue being a pastor I lacked the absolute confidence that God was saying, "Go." I kept throwing obstacles in the way, and they kept getting tossed aside. Finally, I tried one more thing.

All the time we had been on camp staff I had needed only blue jeans and plaid shirts. I had nothing to wear as a pastor, but then I hadn't needed it either. So one day I said, "Okay, Lord, if you want me to be their pastor you will have to provide clothes to wear because I have nothing." I spoke to no one else about my prayer.

One of the common occurrences at camp was people bringing used clothing to donate. Often they were pretty "broken in" already, but sometimes there were some nice items as well. It was fairly common to find a decent shirt or pair of slacks in the "missionary barrel," as we affectionately called it. But the weekend after I prayed I was not prepared for what happened.

I was told that there were clothes at the camp laundry for anyone who needed them. What I found were a dozen designer sweaters, a dozen sport coats, and two dozen dress shirts, and they all fit me. No slacks. But, then, I didn't need them. Someone had already given me $200 to buy them. That was it. We were going to Port Huron, Michigan, to pastor. The church couldn't really pay us enough, but they did provide a parsonage, along with the modest salary. We really had to trust God for any extras or unexpected needs.

But in a sense the financial issue was my own doing. When I was interviewed for the pastoral position I refused to discuss salary until the very end of the process. Earlier one of the committee members had asked, "Don't you want to know what the salary is?" I said no. I did not want consideration of the amount they could pay me to interfere with my decision about whether God wanted us at Westhaven Baptist Church. If he were in it, he would meet our needs, regardless of what they could pay me. I had no clue the extent to which that would be true.

The entire time we were their pastoral family we continued

driving that old Dodge Grand Caravan I mentioned in the previous chapter, with lots of miles on it, and one day the transmission choked. It would go in reverse, and first gear, but that was it. We had no money for car repairs, having a total of exactly $300 in the bank. I called transmission shops, describing the vehicle and the symptoms, and asked for a best guess at what it could run us. Every shop had basically the same answer: "Start at $600 and go up from there."

After multiple calls I was pretty discouraged. I decided it was time to talk to the Lord about the situation (which I should have done in the first place, as my wife always points out). I reminded the Lord about His promise to provide, and then I again remembered James's admonition, "If any of you lack wisdom, let him ask God" (James 1:5). I have absolutely worn out that promise in my life.

I prayed, "Lord, what do I do? The transmission is out in the van, and we don't have the money shops are telling us it will take to fix it. What do I do?"

A thought, definitely not a voice, came to me: "Call Chuck Sinnott." Chuck, a member of our congregation, worked at a car dealership in town, and at first blush calling him might sound like a good idea. But ours was a Chrysler product, and Chuck was a GM parts manager. He wouldn't be able to help me with anything to do with repairing our transmission. Maybe God was omniscient, but apparently He didn't understand car repairs.

"Lord, this doesn't make any sense. Chuck can't help me with this," I objected, but the thought wouldn't go away. I remembered the part in James about not wavering after you ask for and get wisdom. Wisdom is about making a decision, and I needed help. I decided that at least Chuck could give me advice.

I called him at work and explained the situation. "I know you can't help me with this being a Chrysler vehicle, but do you have any advice?"

"Have you called the Chrysler dealer in St. Clair?" he asked. His question didn't seem to make any sense. There was a Chrysler dealership much closer in Port Huron.

"No, Chuck, but I can't afford to take this to a dealer for repair." I expected their rates would be even higher than those of a tranny shop, and my puny $300 bank account hung before my eyes.

"Call the Chrysler dealer in St. Clair." The tone in his voice was emphatic. There was an awkward moment of silence, because I didn't know how to respond. Didn't he hear me say I couldn't afford a dealer to repair it?

"Okay. Thanks, Chuck," and I hung up.

I'll have to admit that when I got off the phone I was pretty aggravated, but not at Chuck. "Lord, this doesn't make any sense!" I protested after I hung up. "I can't afford to go to a dealership!" I think I may have been more hurt than aggravated. Is this what faith produces? Answers that can't be right?

But Chuck's admonition was backed up by James's warning: a double-minded man cannot expect to receive anything from the Lord (James 1:8). I sure didn't want to put myself in the "unprovided for" category because I had asked for wisdom without following the counsel I had received. I dutifully called the Chrysler dealership in St. Clair, already anticipating a fruitless conversation. So much for great faith.

I got the service manager on the phone and explained what vehicle we had, which engine was in it, and what the problem was, but saying nothing about my impressive $300 bankroll. What happened next still gives me tingles when I remember it.

He responded, "It's interesting you called. We have that very transmission lying on our shop floor, but it isn't ours. One of our mechanics bought a van with that engine and transmission, but all he wanted was the engine. I will let you talk to him."

I went through all the information once again with the mechanic, and he verified that it was the correct transmission. I took a breath. "What would it cost for you to do the job?" I asked, fully prepared to need a miracle to cover the cost.

I got one.

"How about $150 for the transmission, and $150 to put it in?" I don't remember the rest of the conversation because I was so shocked. I do know I told him we would bring it down, but I couldn't even afford to have it towed. I ended up driving it all 12 miles to St. Clair in first gear.

There is one more thing I remember clearly. When I got off the phone I am not ashamed to say I danced around the den. I had called on the Lord asking for wisdom, and He had answered. This was not man's doing. Chuck knew nothing about what was going on at the St. Clair Chrysler dealership service department. He could have directed me to the Port Huron dealership. The mechanic did not know how much money I had.

But the Lord knew all of it. He used Scripture, and the mind and voice of a man, to tell me exactly what to do, just the same as He had done countless times in the past through prophets of old.

CHAPTER 15

That You May Be Healed

"Therefore, confess your sins to one another and pray for one another, that you may be healed. The prayer of a righteous person has great power as it is working." James 5:16

One aspect of prayer I wish I understood better, and was more effective in, is prayer for healing. My heart goes out to those who suffer, and I know this was front and center in the public ministry of Jesus. It may be the least powerful dimension of my own prayer life, but I have seen its effect on others.

While we were a missionary family in northern Michigan, we were also part of a local church congregation. I served the congregation on a pulpit supply basis on many occasions while they were searching for a new pastor, and even filled in as an unofficial elder. Eventually they called a new pastor.

I was asked to accompany him to the home of an elderly couple within the congregation, Earl and Ruth Webb. They were about the sweetest couple you could hope to meet, and Earl's health had been deteriorating for years. He had been on oxygen for as long as I had known them, but he had now become confined to a hospital bed in his own home. Ruth had been doing her best to care for him, but he had grown so weak he appeared to be near death.

Although I had received some pastoral education in Bible school, nothing had prepared me for such a visit. I really had no idea what to expect, and all I was told was that we were going to the Webb home to pray for Earl. I would let Pastor James take the lead. We were there with one or two other church leaders.

Lack of effective training in prayer became acutely obvious to the original disciples of Jesus. They had never experienced anything like the power and impact of the ministry of the Messiah. Was that something that only elite individuals in Scripture, like Elijah and Elisha, and others cut from that same bolt of cloth, could manifest? It soon became clear to the twelve disciples that there was a direct correlation between Jesus' ministry power and an effective prayer life.

Finally, one of His disciples got up the courage to talk to Him about it. "Now Jesus was praying in a certain place, and when he finished, one of his disciples said to him, 'Lord, teach us to pray, as John taught his disciples'" (Luke 11:1).

What followed that request is what we now refer to as the Lord's Prayer. That is a bit of a misnomer, because we never read of Jesus praying like this in any other scenario recorded in the New Testament. In reality, it is the Lord's prayer model for the disciples. My purpose is not to lead into an examination and exposition of the principles of prayer expressed in this model, but only to say that the disciples and Jesus Himself recognized the need to teach God-followers how to pray.

We gathered around Earl's hospital bed, and I let the others lead out in prayer. As I said, I had never participated in prayer for healing with someone who was dying. But what I quickly realized was that healing was not what was being prayed for.

There was praise for the work God had done in and through the lives of Earl and Ruth, and thanks for the hope we have in Christ over the power of death and the grave in resurrection. There was the request for God's grace as they faced this dark hour in their lives. And those things are good and meant to be comforting to the sick person and family.

But I suddenly found my mind racing. What was I going to say when it came my turn to pray? I sensed in my spirit that I was not there to wish Earl "bon voyage" as we pushed his boat off toward that "far distant shore." I might betray my ignorance and immaturity in not knowing how to pray, but I knew I could not pray as those before me had done, in spite of their good intentions of comfort. And then it was my turn. Others may have been led to offer prayers of encouragement, but I was going to pray for healing.

As I opened my mouth I suddenly felt a rush of the sense of the presence of the Lord. The words, not in some strange tongue, but fully understandable, poured out. Words of hope, comfort, and encouragement, yes, but much more. I found myself taking authority over sickness and affliction in Earl, rebuking any destruction the enemy of our souls might be working against him and his wife. I have no idea how many minutes elapsed; then, as quickly and suddenly as it had come, that prayer urge was gone. For me the experience was surreal, and even those who had prayed before me wondered what had just happened.

I wish I could say that Earl was totally and immediately healed and that he jumped out of the hospital bed, but not so. However, the next day he began to improve, and the next, and the next, and he continued to improve until he was back to the strength I had always known him to have. He was still on the oxygen, but he was no longer hindered as he had been in those dark moments. And best of all, the radiance in Ruth's face returned after what God had done in restoring her husband to her.

God gave them two more years together, and when the time of darkness once again came to their home, I had a sense of peace in my spirit that this was not a time to pray for restoration to life on the earth, but for graduation to life beyond.

Now someone could easily respond with skepticism and maintain that the reversal in Earl's health had taken place on a purely psychological basis—that Earl's depression and sickness had simply overwhelmed him to the point that he had given up. I could not disprove that hypothesis. At the same time, having been there and witnessed what happened before and after, I do not believe that Earl just needed a shot of encouragement in the arm.

Does God heal only partially, or completely? Does the ministry of Jesus display a kind of huckster approach, a sleight of hand that only appears to produce that which was promised?

In reality, not a single person whom Jesus healed was completely healed. All of these persons carried in their bodies the outworking of death as the natural, inevitable result of sin. Regardless of whether Jesus healed a blind person's sight or a paralytic's back, all eventually died, because their bodies gave out. Consistently, then, Jesus' healing affected only one aspect of that person's need, and the results were in a sense temporary. Earl recovered enough for himself and Ruth to enjoy two more years together, but he still ultimately passed away because of a worn-out body. Could his near-death experience have been the consequence of depression and discouragement, reversed by passionate positivity? I don't believe that to have been the case, but I could not prove it.

So, what about a significant healing verified by a doctor? Let me tell you about someone I will call Susan. I use an alias only because this happened over 24 years ago, and I have no means to contact her for permission to use her real name.

Susan was not a member of our congregation but had no pastor of her own to turn to. She called my office one day, desperate for help, and asked if I would counsel her. I agreed. She had several issues we had to work through, one of which was an injury to her left shoulder. She constantly carried her arm in a sling.

When I asked about the cause, she explained that she worked at a large retail store and had needed assistance from a stockman to retrieve a large boxed item from a top shelf. Susan was quite short and even with a ladder could not safely reach the box to retrieve it for a customer. She called for assistance.

But no stockman came, and after several minutes Susan decided to try to get the box down anyway. It ended up being more than she could handle, and it fell on her shoulder, doing considerable damage to the soft tissue and nerves. The result was some extensive work by a neurosurgeon to repair the damage.

But the surgery was only partially successful, and Susan was left with a great deal of pain and an inability to use the arm. Without complete healing of the shoulder she was unable to get a doctor's release to return to work, and having been recently divorced she was rapidly becoming destitute. Susan pleaded with the doctor, but the surgeon's response was limited to, "I have done everything I can for you. You will have to live with the pain the way it is."

"What am I going to do, pastor?" she asked, and I was ashamed I had no good answer.

About that time a friend took pity on her and paid her way to a ladies' retreat. At the conclusion of a plenary session a woman stood up in the group and announced that God had given her the gift of healing. If there were any women present who would like prayer for healing, they were welcome to seek her out. Susan immediately knew she needed to talk to her about the shoulder injury. But as quickly as that occurred to her, another woman came to mind, someone who had hurt her deeply.

Susan was aware that this other woman was at the retreat, and Susan had held a grudge against her ever since the offense had taken place. The same Scripture that started this chapter teaches, "Therefore, confess your sins to one another and pray for one another, that you may be healed. The prayer of a righteous person has great power as it is working" (James 5:16). Susan knew that she had sinned against this woman by holding the grudge. The Lord wanted Susan to seek reconciliation and forgive the other woman before she went for healing.

It was difficult and awkward, but Susan was faithful to go to the offender, and then afterward sought out the woman who had the gift of healing.

The woman had Susan stand and laid hands on her back, starting at the top of Susan's spine. She began praying while slowly working her hands down the spine. Susan said that as the woman moved down her spine she could feel heat coming from her hands, and Susan could feel her vertebrae moving and popping. It took 45 minutes for the hands to move from top to bottom. When the woman finished, Susan's shoulder was healed.

"Look at this, pastor!" she exclaimed to me, and swung her arm in a full 360-degree circle. "No pain!" She was nearly giddy.

"Have you gone back to your doctor?" I asked. "Yes," Susan said, "I went back to the neurosurgeon, and she examined me. When she finished the surgeon said to me, 'I have no explanation for this, except to say God has healed you.' She gave me the release to go back to work!"

I left one detail out of Susan's healing intentionally, until now. The woman who prayed for Susan prayed in tongues. And why did I do that? Because I used to be in the camp that opposed tongues speaking, and I knew that some of my readers would get to that point in the story and write off the rest of it.

I do not speak in tongues, though I have repeatedly sought the Lord about the matter. I believe that others have the gift and use it properly. But the Holy Spirit gives and withholds gifts as He determines best.

Is it really necessary to forgive others in order to be healed? I can only respond to that by sharing my own story.

Before we moved to Port Huron to pastor Westhaven, I developed an infection that had to be treated with antibiotics. I got a prescription in northern Michigan and started the regimen, but when the antibiotic ran out I was no better. I went to another doctor once we had moved into Port Huron and got a second, stronger antibiotic, but ultimately with the same result.

The doctor told me he was going to prescribe a very strong antibiotic but that we were really running out of options. If this did not remove the infection, we might be looking at serious issues to be dealt with.

There was a pastoral seminar I wanted to attend near Detroit. A long trip in the car was uncomfortable, but I went anyway. In one of the sessions the speaker made a point of connecting healing with forgiveness, and the Lord brought to my mind that I had been harboring bitterness against my father for decades. I mulled it over for the rest of the seminar, and as I started home I realized I had to forgive him.

The apostle Paul wrote, "Children, obey your parents in the Lord, for this is right. 'Honor your father and mother' (this is the first commandment with a promise), 'that it may go well with you and that you may live long in the land'" (Ephesians 6:1-3).

I was driving up the onramp for the expressway and knew this moment was as good as any. I had no sooner forgiven my father that I felt the change in my body—my infection and it symptoms were gone.

CHAPTER 16

Bitterness, Grass, and a Hayride

Reaching the end of hope, she packed a bag and drove to the north woods of Michigan. As the tall pines and aspens began to dominate the scenery, she anticipated the likelihood she would never see them again. And as I waited for the ladies retreat to begin almost 200 miles north, I had no idea that it would be a matter of life or death for her. But God knew, and he was about to use me in an unexpected way, without my even being aware of what was happening.

A critical aspect of a personal relationship with God is becoming sensitive to the prompting of the Holy Spirit. Many Christians talk about the indwelling of the Holy Spirit, but few understand or develop that dimension of the Christian life. This is a tragic reason the church is in the regressive condition evident in many locations around the world.

It is one of the roles of the Spirit to direct us into ministry opportunities and then move through us to meet needs, either naturally or supernaturally. Without that prompting I would almost certainly have missed being used by the Lord to save a life.

One of my favorite activities of camp ministry was driving hayrides into the woods. I would nearly always stop at our west gate and retell the West Side fire story our founder had experienced. The camp would have been overrun by a wildfire except for the intervention of a firefighter on a bulldozer. Except there were no firefighters on bulldozers with fire plows in that area. When our founder followed the tracks into the woods after the forest fire, they ended with no apparent explanation for where the equipment had gone.

But after a couple of years I decided that as a storyteller I needed to come up with new material of my own. So I started using visual aids from nature to illustrate spiritual truths. One story was—and remains—my favorite to share, in part because of what happened on one of the hayrides in response.

It was not a perfect day for a hayride. The sky to the west was completely clouded over, and the air was heavy with moisture. But I doubt that even an impending locust plague could have kept those ladies from clambering aboard the three large hay wagons behind our big four-wheel-drive Ford tractor. Let's just say these otherwise demure women came a little unhinged at camp for the weekend, stuffing straw in sweatshirts and hiding plastic spiders and rubber rats in each other's bunks. This was the place to unwind a little—and laugh a lot.

As we headed out into the forest I could feel a mist beginning to fall, and I started praying that God would hold off the rain long enough to get the hayride back in. I realized that this afternoon's hayride might not be the right time to stop and tell one of those stories. At the same time I sensed a tug on my heart to do so anyway, and I began to pray for wisdom about what to do.

When we got to the place where I had planned to tell the story it was still not raining, and I sensed an urgency to tell it. I pulled the tractor to a stop in a location that would allow me to be visible to all the ladies on the three trailers. I bent down, plucked a stalk of grass with the seeds on it, and prepared to tell my story, . . . but something was wrong.

Instead of quieting down to listen to me, the ladies were starting to giggle and whisper to one another. "Okay, what's so funny?"

I asked them, hoping it wasn't something embarrassing about my attire. "Look behind you!" they responded.

Directly behind me about ten feet away in his brush blind was a deer hunter in full camo. It was bow season, and I hadn't seen him at all. "Sorry," I said. "I won't be long." But he stomped off through the woods while the ladies howled with laughter. I wondered how on earth I could get a lid on it now.

But they did eventually stop laughing, and I was able to continue. "Can anyone tell me what this is?" and I held up the stalk with the seeds dangling. "Grass," several offered, and I said, "Yes, grass seed on a stalk. Now look around. Can any of you tell me where the grass started and spread out from to cover the ground?" Of course they could not, so I continued.

"Bitterness is anger gone to seed. Anger in and of itself is not bad. Anger is like an emotional sense of touch. If you put your fingers against something hot the sensation warns you to pull them away before you get burned. Anger warns you of emotional danger. It is your soul touching something that can hurt you. If you deal with it immediately you can protect yourself. But let anger simmer, and it goes to seed as bitterness. Pretty soon it spreads, and eventually you can't tell where it started. It just permeates your life.

"The apostle Paul warned, 'Be angry and do not sin; do not let the sun go down on your anger, and give no opportunity to the devil' (Ephesians 4:26).

"When we do not resolve our anger promptly, when we harbor anger it can become bitterness, and we open ourselves to the devil's destructive work in our lives."

The mist was starting to give way to a drizzle, and I knew I needed to get them back before it became rain. We made it back in time before chapel. As I was helping the ladies off the wagons one came close to my ear and shared that my story had been just what she needed to hear. On her face was an earnestness that shocked me.

I put away the tractor and wagons but came back before chapel started to let her know I was concerned and available if she needed to talk. I stood in one of the aisles desperately scanning the large crowd but could not see her. The reason was that she was sitting right beside where I was standing, but I was looking the other way. Although she knew I was looking for her, she was afraid to let me know she was there.

I didn't see her throughout the rest of the retreat, but the next Wednesday night our founder shared a story. After retreats he would stand out on the road leading out of camp to say goodbye to each camper. The previous weekend one lady had left and then returned to tell him her story.

She said, "I got up the road and decided I had to come back to tell you what happened. I packed up my things to come to camp and told the Lord that if he did not speak to me this weekend, after I left camp I was going to commit suicide. Steve told a story in the woods about bitterness, and the Lord showed me my life was full of it. I know I have to go back and forgive those who have hurt me."

I cannot describe what it was like to hear that from our founder. I had been so close to disobeying that prompting of the Holy Spirit. I became good friends with the woman and her husband and saw them many times after that at camp retreats. God did an amazing work of healing in her marriage and life.

I just wish I could tell that hunter how important the loss of his hunting spot was for one lady.

CHAPTER 17

A Tale of Two Pastors

In all my opportunities to minister to the needs of people at camp, none stands out as more surprising than what happened at a pastors' retreat one fall.

It was a gorgeous fall day in Michigan—crisp air, colored leaves littering the ground, and full sunshine in a deep blue sky. But a dark thundercloud hung over one pastor as he sat alone in the dining hall. I prayed the Lord would give me what he needed as I sat down at the table with him.

We talked, and he shared his burden with me. Disagreement had come between him and his co-pastor. For the limited time I had known them I had only seen a great relationship. But this interpersonal conflict was threatening to tear apart not only their friendship but their ministry as well. He was emotionally crushed by what he could see happening.

As I listened to him explain the circumstances of their conflict, it dawned on me that he needed the same advice that someone had given me on handling personal disagreements and conflict. I began to see that what was concerning him was not worth the loss of the relationship with his friend and co-pastor ministry partner.

But sharing my insight meant that I had to tell this pastor he needed to yield his rights on the issue and be reconciled, not an easy task for him if he felt justified in his own position. Nevertheless, the dark cloud seemed to be less ominous over him after I had shared with him that I'd had to do the same thing. I had to move on at that point to other responsibilities, so I prayed with him and left him to ponder and talk over with the Lord what I had told him.

The next day I was floored when this staid middle-aged pastor saw me in the dining hall, jumped up from his table, and literally came leaping and skipping across the room, exclaiming, "I'm free! I'm free!" and throwing his arms around me.

He had realized the truth of what the Lord had prompted me to share with him, understood that the issue was not worth the loss of a friend and ministry partner, and chosen instead to yield his rights and love his brother. I doubt I have ever seen anyone so joyful immediately after having been told he was in the wrong. But he had done business with God, the best possible response to what I shared, and his soul was set free from the burden he had carried with him to camp.

I hadn't told him anything he didn't already understand as a pastor. But sometimes we acquire balls and chains in our own lives so subtly and slowly we don't realize we are dragging them along behind us. Sometimes it just takes a pair of objective eyes, a gentle voice, and the prompting of the Holy Spirit to open the lock that binds those hindrances to us.

If you have to give medicine, it helps to know it works because you have taken it yourself, which in this case I had, in regular doses. One of the most important lessons I have had to repeatedly learn has been the necessity of denying myself to follow Jesus as a disciple. The pastor I had shared with had experienced an overwhelming joy by denying himself and loving his brother in Christ.

CHAPTER 18

That Your Joy May Be Full

The advice I gave the pastor was spiritual refreshment drawn from the same well to which I had been about 14 years earlier. While I was pastoring I was struck by one of the promises of Jesus related to denying self:

> "As the Father has loved me, so have I loved you. Abide in my love. If you keep my commandments, you will abide in my love, just as I have kept my Father's commandments and abide in his love. These things I have spoken to you, that my joy may be in you, and that your joy may be full.
>
> "This is my commandment, that you love one another as I have loved you. Greater love has no one than this, that someone lay down his life for his friends. You are my friends if you do what I command you.'" John 15:9–14

I certainly wanted to be known as a friend of Jesus, so I decided I needed to be more diligent in following Jesus' command to love others. But what was this promise of being full of joy over serving others? I had to admit I really couldn't relate to that aspect of servanthood.

As much as I had tried to help others, I would have to say I had never experienced the level of joy that seems to be indicated in

John 15—"that my joy may be in you, and that your joy may be full." That troubled me. I wanted to understand why that was and what needed to change.

As I sat in my church office early one morning, I decided I would try an experiment. Every person I encountered that day would become a part of that experiment without their being aware of it. For each I would find some kind, encouraging thing to say, without being critical or judgmental in any way. It was then that I discovered one of the obstacles to joy in my life.

I realized that I gave out expressions of kindness and encouragement only when I felt as though people had "earned" them. I had grown up as a perfectionist, and I was very hard on myself. I was subconsciously doing the same thing to others. By breaking that chain, I was about to discover firsthand what "your joy may be full" means.

The first person I saw was my secretary, Jane. I quickly searched for encouraging words and started heaping praise on her for her diligence about the office responsibilities she carried out for me. It was clear from her response that this was exactly what she needed to hear. Her countenance brightened immediately, and as I sat at my desk I had a sense I was on the right track.

The next person I encountered a little while later was a retired man from our congregation. One of the leaders, he loved to just come to the office, sit down, and talk. I struggled on those visits because I had much to do as a pastor, and I didn't always view these morning moments as important in comparison to those items on my "to do" list. Almost on cue, Walt appeared in my office doorway.

I nearly panicked. I had committed to saying kind, encouraging things to every person I met. What could I say to someone I had come to see as an interruption to my busy schedule? In a split second I asked the Lord what to say. And then I noticed something.

"Great tie!" I blurted out. Now I have to admit, I almost felt as though I were lying. I really didn't care for the tie. But it obviously was one he liked, so it was a "great tie" to the person who mattered most. Walt's face lit up, and so did something else.

Joy may be one of the most difficult things in the world to describe. You really have to just experience it to understand it. And I suddenly realized I was experiencing it big time. I was only two people into my experiment and already felt almost dizzy with what "the joy of the LORD is your strength" (Nehemiah 8:10) means on a practical basis. It is *His* joy, manifested in us, just as Jesus said.

I did the same thing with every person I met that day, and the joy intensified with every divine appointment. It was surreal. I almost felt selfish, lavishing expressions of love and kindness on people whether or not they deserved it, knowing that my experience of joy would continue to increase. Ironically, this was about to backfire on me.

The evening of the "experiment" I was so caught up with what was happening that I treated something Audrey was going through flippantly, without realizing that my response might be viewed as uncaring. At the very time I was trying to explain what I was experiencing in my joy experiment, she was angry because of how I had treated her.

She was right in her anger, and I knew I was wrong. I had matured enough spiritually by then to know as soon as I recognized I had offended someone (especially my wife) that I needed to repent, admit my fault, seek forgiveness with genuine remorse, and be reconciled. But there was a problem I never in a million years could have foreseen.

I was filled with so much joy that I felt as though I would explode. I was being pulled emotionally in two totally opposite directions at the same time. Although I knew in my head that I needed to be remorseful, I could not manifest remorse. Even the action of expressing love to my wife by seeking forgiveness for having offended her brought joy to me.

Shame and sorrow suck the life out of, . . . well, life. When Israel returned from exile under the leadership of Nehemiah and Ezra, there was much to be ashamed and sorrowful about. At the reading of the Law, the new inhabitants of Jerusalem were cut to the heart by their failures to obey and honor Yahweh. We are told that their response was to burst into tears as the depth of their transgressions was revealed:

> "And Nehemiah, who was the governor, and Ezra the priest and scribe, and the Levites who taught the people said to all the people, 'This day is holy to the LORD your God; do not mourn or weep.' For all the people wept as they heard the words of the Law. Then he said to them, 'Go your way. Eat the fat and drink sweet wine and send portions to anyone who has nothing ready, for this day is holy to our LORD. And do not be grieved, for the joy of the LORD is your strength.'" Nehemiah 8:9-10

Before I came to know Christ as my Savior, I sought pleasure as a means to cope with the emptiness, frustration, and sorrow I experienced. But pleasure doesn't hold a candle to joy. Notice that in verse 10, above, the people were instructed to not be grieved over their failures but instead to celebrate what had been done for them. More importantly, they were to look to the needs of those around them. The consequence would be joy. And the next verses tell us they got it:

> "So the Levites calmed all the people, saying, 'Be quiet, for this day is holy; do not be grieved.' And all the people went their way to eat and drink and to send portions and to make great rejoicing, because they had understood the words that were declared to them." Nehemiah 8:11-12

It may well be that one of the most visible manifestations of weak spiritual life comes from a lack of understanding the meaning of "the joy of the LORD is your strength."

One of the saddest realities for "nones," in my opinion, is that they have never gotten to experience that level of spiritual strength or know that kind of joy.

CHAPTER 19

No Secrets

Does God really speak to people today, or is this perception really just our imaginations on overdrive based on "fables" from the Old Testament?

Omniscience is the one-hundred-dollar word theologians throw around to talk about how much God knows. They argue about just what his knowledge involves and how far it extends. Sometimes the Bible offers even semi-comical anecdotes on the subject. For example:

> "Once when the king of Syria was warring against Israel, he took counsel with his servants, saying, 'At such and such a place shall be my camp.' But the man of God [Elisha] sent word to the king of Israel, 'Beware that you do not pass this place, for the Syrians are going down there.' And the king of Israel sent to the place about which the man of God told him. Thus he used to warn him, so that he saved himself there more than once or twice.
>
> "And the mind of the king of Syria was greatly troubled because of this thing, and he called his servants and said to them, 'Will you not show me who of us is for the king of Israel?' And one of his servants said, 'None, my lord, O king; but Elisha, the prophet who is in Israel, tells the king of Israel the words that you speak in your bedroom.'" 2 Kings 6:8–12

This is an amusing tale of a frustrated king of Syria trying to make war against the northern ten tribes known as Israel. No sooner would he make a battle plan than the prophet Elisha would perceive it and warn the king of Israel. A little background material would be helpful for those unfamiliar with the Old Testament prophets.

The story from 2 Kings is written in such a lighthearted fashion that it is hard to take seriously. But the crux of the issue for me is that I have experienced this very scenario in my journey with the Lord.

Multiple times.

Pastoring a local church did not turn out to be the dream come true I had always hoped it would be. I gleaned the basic Bible study, theology, and preaching skills I needed from my years at school. But I lacked many of the personal and situational skills I needed, and it quickly became clear that being a pastor of a small transitional church was not a good fit for me.

After two years of stress with no clear vision that the trend was going to to change for me, I finally concluded that it was time for me to leave—time for the church to get another pastor. My wife and I began seeking the Lord's leading elsewhere.

We did try candidating at a couple of other churches in case the problem was simply that we could not meet the needs where we were. But there was no sense of peace for us that the Lord was directing us to those congregations either. I wondered about the possibility of returning to our previous ministry in Christian camping, and after checking I discovered the door was open.

All of this was done without our giving any indication to anyone at our church that we were considering leaving that ministry. We weren't trying to put pressure on the church to change in order to keep us, and we did not want the members to sense that we were ungrateful for the opportunity they had given us to test the waters of pastoral ministry. We felt it was best to wait until we had a clear sense of direction from the Lord. We were very careful and certain that no one knew of our anticipated plans.

But Someone did.

I determined to make the announcement after one of our congregation's quarterly business meeting. Things went smoothly for the dinner and meeting, and then at the end I broke the news gently, much to the astonishment of those who were there. But it was old news to two of those attending.

People lined up to tell me how surprised and saddened they were that we would be leaving. But the last lady stepped forward and floored me. Our leaving had already been announced to her and her husband—but not by a human being.

Linda Dahn and her husband, Jim, were two of the most involved members of our congregation. Both wore multiple hats, and Linda was probably one of our most active prayer warriors. They had been on vacation the week before the business meeting, but Linda had still been faithful to her prayers for our church. As she prayed for me and our family, she got a totally unexpected response from the Lord: "The McCormicks are going back to camp." Linda was stunned.

She turned to Jim and told him what she thought the Lord had just said to her. He was incredulous. "No way!" He had not heard anything to that effect, and if neither Jim nor Linda knew, no one else in our congregation could have.

Linda described her reaction to my announcement: "My first thought was to talk to you and confirm to you that God was leading you back to camp. I love confirmation myself so wanted to pass that on to you."

When I stood and made the announcement she was as shocked as I was at the confirmation of her encounter with the Lord during her prayer time. She waited until everyone else had gone through the "Sorry to hear that" line of well-wishers and then dropped a bombshell of her own on me. I had been so careful. Not one person in the congregation was aware of our intended change of ministry direction. I believe the Lord spilled the beans so we could know for certain we were following His leading.

Perhaps that story does not have enough specific detail to satisfy some that it was a genuine encounter with the Lord. But how about being told to be somewhere at the exact minute something was going to take place, something you knew nothing about?

CHAPTER 20

A Word Behind You

What would you do if God were to tell you to go stand out in the woods at exactly midnight because something was going to happen that you needed to be there for?

The prophet Isaiah had one of the most prolifically blessed writing ministries of all the prophets of Israel. The accuracy level of his descriptions of things and events in the future that had been revealed to him is at times off the chart. Specific accounts of events centuries before their occurrence reveal a supernatural hand at work in space and time.

His description of renewed spiritual life in the people of God in the kingdom age is perhaps most striking. One such statement is particularly interesting: "Your ears shall hear a word behind you, saying, 'This is the way, walk in it,' when you turn to the right or when you turn to the left" (Isaiah 30:21). This can't be realistic, can it? The notion that when God restored all things he would personally be involved, directing the lives of His people by speaking to them, sounds like fairytale material.

At least that is what I thought at one time.

While we were active in camping ministry we worked with youth predominately, and more specifically with the teen workers who would come to help mow grass, serve meals, cut firewood and, so forth. They were a great bunch of kids, and those were the best years of my ministry experience.

But kids will be kids, and, of course, camp being camp, one of the un-programmed activities was sneaking out at night. Not only could these kids get into trouble doing things they should not, but the risk of injury was all too real. The general camp policy was that they were not to be outdoors after lights out in the evening.

But to put teeth into the requirement for those who participated in our program, we added a specific rule: if any members of our crew were caught outside their housing unit after lights out without informing their counselors of a valid need to do so, they would be required to call a parent in the morning to come pick up the teenager and go home. This was a rule I hoped I would never have to enforce.

On Thursday nights we would have a cookout for our crew, with the typical fare of hotdogs, hamburgers, and everything that goes along with them. While the food was being prepared we had a lot of informal games going on, or just sitting around talking and relaxing.

I really enjoyed this time with the teens when I could get it. This was not often because Thursday night was also time to spend with my own family—a wife and now five daughters. But for whatever reason, one Thursday afternoon I was with the crew on a ball diamond while the hotdogs and hamburgers cooked, and several of us were throwing Frisbees. In those days I could accurately throw a Frisbee a long way, so the guys I was throwing with were backed up clear across the ball field in several directions.

Suddenly I heard a voice from behind instructing me, "You need to be outside staff house tonight at midnight." To this day I believe it was an actual voice. It was so clear and distinct it prompted me to look all around me, but no one was there. I wondered what on earth could have happened. Staff house was where our crew stayed.

I went home and told my wife about it. She was as dumbfounded as I. We had a great crew that week and didn't anticipate any issues. "What are you going to do?" she asked.

"I don't know," I responded. "I guess I'll be outside the staff house at midnight."

I didn't relish the idea of giving up sleep to follow up on such a crazy occurrence. I needed my rest as much as any of the summer crew. But I decided to be outside the housing unit by 11:30 since I wasn't sure whether "midnight" was supposed to be literal. I would put up with the mosquitos for as little time as necessary. I positioned myself in the bushes near an outdoor light where I had a pretty good view of all entrances to our building.

I started to feel like a complete idiot by about 11:40, swatting away mosquitos, when off to my right I saw a figure emerging from the darkness, and my heart skipped a beat. That direction was toward the Huron National Forest, and the fence line was only about a hundred yards away. I had not seen any cars or flashlights, so I knew someone was trying to sneak around undetected.

The intruder was dressed in black from head to toe and crept quietly up to the back of the building below the windows to the girls' housing section. I could hardly believe what was happening. My mind began racing as I tried to figure out what my plan of action had to be. The shape was about the size of a lightweight adult. I was young and strong and felt I could tackle whomever it was if I had to.

Silently the person moved on before stopping directly under the light at one of the doors to the boys' housing. "This is nuts!" I thought. By then I could see that it was clearly a guy in a hoodie, with no weapons of any kind, listening at the door. He rounded the end of the building and headed to our dining hall. That was when I decided to catch up with and confront him.

He turned out he was just one of the staff family kids. There wasn't any policy that he couldn't be in camp at night, but I didn't want him messing around outside the housing unit for my crew, so I just sent him home. I would decide whether to talk to his parents later. I looked at my watch: 11:45. I wondered if that was all I was supposed to be there for. But the word "midnight" stuck in my head. I really wanted to go home to sleep, but I returned to the bushes for 15 minutes more.

At the stroke of midnight, the back door of the boy's housing unit opened, and out came my best worker, Chad Cutshall. My heart sank. He was the epitome of the kind of kid I wanted on the crew. In fact, I had asked him to spend a major chunk of the summer on our crew because he was big, a hard worker, and so well liked. I caught up with Chad in the driveway.

"What are you doing?" came out of the dark behind him. I thought he would jump out of his skin. He was as astonished to see me as I was to see him out of the staff house.

We walked to the dining hall, and he told me he had been planning to meet the staff kid I had just sent home. They were friends intending to go down to the lake to "look at the stars." What they were going to do was irrelevant to me at that moment. "You know the rule, don't you?" He hung his head, "Yes," he admitted, looking at the floor. "In the morning I will meet you at the office, and you will call your dad to pick you up."

Although I talked to the director about what had happened and got his advice, I knew I had no choice. I could not appear to be playing favorites if the rule were to be taken seriously. Even so, my decision was extremely unpopular among the summer staff.

Before the two left I spoke to Chad's father, a friend of mine. "Watch his attitude this week. If he is genuinely remorseful for breaking the rule, I will let him come back." And that is how it worked out. This was an important learning experience in his life. But that is not the end of the story.

As a consequence of sending Chad home, someone else with a guilty conscience came forward. I became aware of other things that had gone on that night that were also outside the rules. I followed up on that information, confirmed it, and dealt with it as well.

All of this occurred as a result of a very clear and specific statement that had seemingly come out of thin air: "You need to be outside the staff house at midnight." I believe it was the Lord. No other explanation makes sense.

But there had been nothing serious about the things I had discovered. No violence or harm to anyone, nothing stolen, and no sexual impropriety had taken place. So why would the Lord have prompted me to be there? At face value all of this was just kids being kids.

But I knew there had to be more. First, it served as a warning to all who heard about the incident that I was serious about enforcing the rule and didn't play favorites. Who knows what else might have happened, with more serious consequences, based on someone deciding to be out and about in the middle of the night? Second, it had an impact in Chad's life, as he learned he needed to follow expectations as someone whom others viewed as an example. Third, it made me aware that even great kids could be tempted to do things they shouldn't, and I needed to be more watchful of all those under my care.

And finally, I realized that my ministry could and would be directed in a very precise way if I were to remain sensitive and obedient to the prompting of the Holy Spirit.

How much might we detect or become aware of if we are open to hearing from the Lord? How much loss or tragedy might we escape, or save others from, if we were more discerning of the Holy Spirit? I only know what took place when I responded to what happened on the ball field. It was surreal. I had never experienced an instruction quite like that from the Lord before, but it would not be the last time. I was also to learn that caution is necessary.

Scripture warns believers about communication with the spiritual realm. The apostle John wrote,

"Beloved, do not believe every spirit, but test the spirits to see whether they are from God, for many false prophets have gone out into the world. By this you know the Spirit of God: every spirit that confesses that Jesus Christ has come in the flesh is from God, and every spirit that does not confess Jesus is not from God. This is the spirit of the antichrist, which you heard was coming and now is in the world already." 1 John 4:1-3

The Bible identifies at least four or five types of spiritual beings, besides God himself, that live in that dimension, and not all have our best interests in mind. Even Satan "disguises himself as an angel of light" (2 Corinthians 11:14). Learning to discern among spiritual sources, and avoiding communication that does not come from the Lord, are both paramount when learning to walk in the Spirit and seek the Lord's guidance. While adequately teaching that process is beyond the scope of this book, James gives valuable instruction on the subject in James 3:13-18:

"Who is wise and understanding among you? By his good conduct let him show his works in the meekness of wisdom. But if you have bitter jealousy and selfish ambition in your hearts, do not boast and be false to the truth. This is not the wisdom that comes down from above, but is earthly, unspiritual, demonic. For where jealousy and selfish ambition exist, there will be disorder and every vile practice. But the wisdom from above is first pure, then peaceable, gentle, open to reason, full of mercy and good fruits, impartial and sincere. And a harvest of righteousness is sown in peace by those who make peace."

I had for several years been sensitive to anything that had come to me from the spirit realm. I needed to learn to be open to the good, while at the same time avoiding the evil of that dimension. I had known that my life had to change but not precisely what had to change or how to effect that change. The bottom line was that I would not become more consistent in avoiding sin in my own life until I learned to obey the promptings of the Holy Spirit. Paul wrote of this reality to the Christians at Rome:

> "For God has done what the law, weakened by the flesh, could not do. By sending his own Son in the likeness of sinful flesh and for sin, he condemned sin in the flesh, in order that the righteous requirement of the law might be fulfilled in us, who walk not according to the flesh but according to the Spirit. For those who live according to the flesh set their minds on the things of the flesh, but those who live according to the Spirit set their minds on the things of the Spirit. For to set the mind on the flesh is death, but to set the mind on the Spirit is life and peace. For the mind that is set on the flesh is hostile to God, for it does not submit to God's law; indeed, it cannot. Those who are in the flesh cannot please God." Romans 8:3-8

Paul taught the same thing to the church at Galatia:

> "But I say, walk by the Spirit, and you will not gratify the desires of the flesh. For the desires of the flesh are against the Spirit, and the desires of the Spirit are against the flesh, for these are opposed to each other, to keep you from doing the things you want to do . . . If we live by the Spirit, let us also keep in step with the Spirit." Galatians 5:16-17, 25

Thus, it is the role of the Holy Spirit to actively lead the children in obedience to God's will. This wasn't something Paul dreamed up on his own. It had been promised in Ezekiel 36:26-27:

> "I will give you a new heart, and a new spirit I will put within you. And I will remove the heart of stone from your flesh and

give you a heart of flesh. And I will put my Spirit within you, and cause you to walk in my statutes and be careful to obey my rules."

This prompting is intended to not only keep us from walking in sin but to direct us in fulfilling our ministry callings, . . . and sometimes in unusual ways.

The Holy Spirit instructed Philip to chase down an Ethiopian official in his chariot as he was about to leave Jerusalem. Philip overheard him reading Scripture and used the opportunity to lead the man to faith in Jesus (Acts 8:26-40).

In a church I had never before attended, a man whom I had never met walked directly up to me and shook my hand. He had prophetic gifting, and the Holy Spirit prompted him to communicate a personal message to me. He identified my spiritual gifting, the level of it, and what my ministry calling had been for a couple of decades. He referred to a longing I had to move into another level of ministering in the power of the Spirit, something I had prayed much about. He spoke of a future event in which I would do the very thing I had always wanted to do. There can be no human, materialistic explanation for how he knew the details of the secrets of my heart.

Yes, God still speaks to people today, because he has children to raise, direct, and even chasten, as I will touch on in the next chapter.

CHAPTER 21

Those He Loves as Sons

One of the most important aspects of God's personal working and communication in the lives of his children is ironically one of the least favorite: chastening.

"Have you forgotten the exhortation that addresses you as sons?

"'My son, do not regard lightly the discipline of the Lord,
    nor be weary when reproved by him.
For the Lord disciplines the one he loves,
    and chastises every son whom he receives.'

"It is for discipline that you have to endure. God is treating you as sons. For what son is there whom his father does not discipline? If you are left without discipline, in which all have participated, then you are illegitimate children and not sons. Besides this, we have had earthly fathers who disciplined us and we respected them. Shall we not much more be subject to the Father of spirits and live? For they disciplined us for a short time as it seemed best to them, but he disciplines us for our good, that we may share his holiness. For the moment all discipline seems painful rather than pleasant, but later it yields the peaceful fruit of righteousness to those who have been trained by it." Hebrews 12:5–11

I know I could fill more than one volume with examples of the Lord's work to discipline me as a son. Sometimes that has taken the form of reproof or rebuke from another brother or sister in Christ. Sometimes it has involved His direct intervention in my life, even preventing words from emerging from my mouth that would not have been helpful.

Jesus said, "'If your brother sins against you, go and tell him his fault, between you and him alone. If he listens to you, you have gained your brother'" (Matthew 18:15). This is one of the most important, and neglected, principles of life in the body of Christ. Failure to understand and properly implement it is one of the leading causes of division in the church. If done correctly it can bring restoration of relationships.

At one time Audrey and I participated in ministry with an elderly couple. Both were very hard workers, and we enjoyed our time with them. Both have since gone on to be with the Lord. But there came a point when I felt I needed to talk to the husband about something that had been brought to my attention.

It was nothing earthshaking or headline worthy. He would bump a cart of pots and pans into boys in the aisle of our dining hall kitchen if the teens in my program were in the way when he was trying to put dishes away. Maybe someone had been disrespectful to him, or maybe he was tired of being ignored. The issue certainly wasn't serious, but whatever the reason I needed to address it and wanted to do it privately.

Both he and his wife were at home when I went to visit. They were an adorable old couple and were very gracious as they invited me in to sit and talk. I felt a little uneasy, as though I were setting up an ambush on the sofa, but I was prepared to be as emphatic as I had to, to convince him that he couldn't continue to do what he had been doing.

But when I opened my mouth, instead of complaint or correction, out came words of praise and appreciation. I talked about how long the two had been on staff and how many teen workers they must have been around over the years. I remarked to him that with all his experience working around teen guys, I would appreciate any insights he might have for me on how to make things work better. I thanked them for their ministry and excused myself to leave.

When I got out on their little porch it was as though I awoke from a dream. I remember saying to myself, "*What was that?*" I hadn't said anything I had intended to say when I walked in. I couldn't really go back inside and try again. But I didn't need to. The most astonishing thing happened.

He was transformed. Never once after that did he bump into any of our guys with the cart, and I hadn't even mentioned it! He didn't need correction—he needed appreciation. Some people open their mouths and stick in a foot. I think that sometimes I just open mine to change feet. But just like Balaam's donkey, I opened my mouth that time, and God filled it with just what that man needed to hear.

The Lord needed to correct my behavior as much as my brother needed to make a change. He needed a gentle word of encouragement. But the Lord knew I wasn't planning to deliver such a message, so He took over.

When the apostle Paul was launched into ministry, the Holy Spirit paired him with Barnabas, whose name meant "son of encouragement." The combination was more important than probably either of them realized. One of the most powerful tools for change in a person's life is encouragement.

CHAPTER 22

Rocking the Boat

Our oldest daughter, Jen, became a missionary herself, with an organization called Youth With a Mission, or YWAM, in 2000. This was a decision that would have a profound impact on our whole family in the years that followed.

She eventually joined the crew of the Mercy Ship Anastasis. At over 500 feet in length, it was at the time the largest nongovernmental organization (NGO) medical ship in the world. The ship had originally been an Italian luxury liner known as the Victoria, but after retirement it had been purchased with donations and converted into a floating hospital staffed over the course of its years of ministry by a total of over 25,000 volunteer doctors, nurses, and crew members. It accommodated "three state-of-the-art operating rooms, a 40-bed hospital ward, a dental clinic, a laboratory, an x-ray unit, and three cargo holds" (www.mercyships.org).

We were proud of our daughter and her work but missed her a lot. This was especially true for me. I was a firstborn son, and Jen, as my own firstborn, and I were a lot alike. We would get stories about where Jen was, usually in Africa, and what she was doing as a missionary. Thousands of poor people in places like Benin would line up for days waiting for the ship to make port and minister to their desperate conditions and afflictions.

Back home during those years we would have over 125 teens and

staff in our summer worker program at camp. I shared Jen's stories with them as encouragement to consider missions themselves.
During the summer of 2001 there was a totally unanticipated consequence to those stories.

Our guy counselors, Matt Brown and Brian Lixey, hatched a
plan. They knew how much I missed Jen, so, unbeknownst to me,
they took it upon themselves to take up a collection among the
teens and from their own pockets that summer. At the end of the
summer camping season they presented me with enough money to
buy a plane ticket to go to see Jen at port in Glasgow, Scotland, when
the ship traveled back to Europe to refit and resupply.

The night before I flew out I was unable to sleep because of the
excitement, and I wasn't able to sleep on the flight over the Atlantic.
The best I could do was put on the sleep mask and lie back in the
seat. I was essentially on autopilot myself as I plodded through the
nearly empty Shiphol airport in the Netherlands in the middle of
the night looking for my next gate and connecting flight. By the
time I got to the customs line at Glasgow I'd had basically no sleep
in 48 hours. My brain felt like the consistency of mashed potatoes,
and I feared having to process questions with answers more complex than yes or no. As I neared the counter I prayed, "Dear God,
just let me get through this checkpoint." The security agent seemed
to eye me suspiciously, with my bloodshot eyes and teetering equi-
librium, but let me pass.

I was officially in Scotland, the land of heather, highlands, kilts,
and the Loc Ness Monster, before it suddenly dawned on me: I had
no idea what to do next.

In the excitement of obtaining a passport, arranging the flight,
and preparing things at home for my absence, I had totally forgotten to make plans for arrival at my destination. I had nowhere to
stay, no contact phone numbers, and no idea how to get to the port,
or even which dock the ship would be at. I felt like a total idiot.

I wandered the airport for at least an hour, and even prayed,

"God, please have someone walk up out of the blue and tell me what to do next." I really believed that God could have bailed me out like that if He had wanted to. But no, He had another plan.

I had been born in England but had never been back, and one of my goals was to travel south, down to the Liverpool area, and see where my mom had grown up and where my life had started. As I drifted through the airport wondering what to do next I noticed a travel store with maps and tourist information. I didn't have anything else to do, so I decided to go into the store and find a map for my much-anticipated trip.

There were quite a few to compare and choose from, and as much as my brain would function in my sleep-deprived state I looked through them. I am amazed I was able to fold them back up properly, but I finally made my selection and went to the counter.

The young lady was a sweet, non-sleep-deprived employee who cheerfully greeted me. She asked about my travel plans in Great Britain, and I mentioned that I was actually there to meet a large medical ship.

"Oh, you mean this one?" she asked. I had to be dreaming.

She reached under the counter and pulled out a photocopied flier. On it was all the information necessary for volunteers who were flying into the country to meet the Anastasis at its berth at King George V Dock the next day. The Lord had chosen to answer my prayer, not by bringing a person to me but by leading me to that person instead. Hallelujah!

I got a room at a motel near the airport and took a taxi to the dock the next day. The ship had arrived only moments before I got dockside. I watched for Jen as they lowered the gangplank and secured the ship. But as many people as I saw, my daughter's face was not among them.

After finding my way to the reception desk, I stood in line, bags in hand, waiting to be greeted any moment by Jen, but still did not see her. As I waited I overheard the receptionist turn to another crew member and say, "Do we have another laminator? This one has stopped working, and we have to get badges ready for our VIP tour of the ship." I thought, "You have to be kidding, Lord."

Back home I was practically known as Mr. Fixit, working on anything and everything around camp, including the laminator in our activities program office. But surely, I hadn't come to Scotland to fix things. All the same, I knew by the panic in her voice that they needed someone on the ship to help them out. I stepped to the counter.

"I don't mean to eavesdrop, but I overheard you say you have a laminator that is not working. I am actually here to meet my daughter, Jennifer, but I could take a look at it for you. I actually fixed one where I work in the States, but I don't have any tools with me." The receptionist didn't hesitate. She got on the PA system and paged, "Any electrician, please bring tools to the reception area and ask for Steve McCormick."

In the PR office where Jen worked, my daughter heard the announcement and turned to a coworker. "Are you kidding me? I haven't even seen my dad yet, and they are already paging him to work on something?" She later admitted to me that she was the one who had broken the laminator. I also found out that the reason for the tension in the reception area was that the main benefactor for the ship was to arrive, and there was to be press present. As it turned out, fixing the jammed laminator was not going to be the only thing I worked on aboard the Anastasis.

It was good to finally get a night's sleep in my cabin. I was really excited to spend some time with Jen, and that day looked ideal for doing some sightseeing. In fact, the crew had already arranged for a tour bus to Edinburgh. Perfect.

Abruptly I heard the ship's captain make an announcement over the PA: "All shore leave is immediately canceled. We have to have enough crew available to load the supplies on the dock." There was a collective groan of crew members around me. Those who were already gone were gone. But those who were still waiting to get on the bus, which included Jen, were stuck. Jen was really disappointed. Anticipation of the months ahead on the ship had primed them to maximize their time ashore.

I had to think fast. Part of me wanted to be with my daughter on an excursion to Edinburgh—which she couldn't do now. The bus would not wait. But the other part of me wanted her to go. I went to the captain and asked whether I could take her place. As a guest I would not have been expected to be part of the loading detail. He agreed that I could do so, and Jen got on the bus. I didn't realize how important for the crew my decision was at that moment. I was just a dad looking out for his daughter.

I joined the crew members on the dock. At 47, and as a mountain biker and weightlifter, I was in very good physical condition. This would be no big deal for me. But the crew member in charge on the dock said they had enough people outside already and asked me to report to the ship's steward inside, where the supplies had to be loaded onto the hold elevator.

Inside, the steward saw my size and informed me that I would be the one to load the elevator. He explained how much the ancient freight elevator could handle, how to load it, how to close the safety gate and door, and how to send it down with a warning shout that it was being lowered.

"But," he cautioned, "if it doesn't go down, then open the door, open the gate, close the gate, close the door, and hit the button again." Hmmm. The ship had been built in 1953, a year before I was born. By 2001, the old freight elevator was flat worn out. This could be interesting.

We took in supplies from the dock as fast as I could load them into the elevator. I reached the elevator capacity, slid the gate closed, shut the door, shouted the warning, and hit the button.

From the bowels of the ship came "Nothing . . ." in response. The elevator hadn't budged. Had I made a mistake?

I opened the door, opened the gate, checked my loading of the goods, shut the gate, shut the door, shouted the warning, and hit the button. Once again came the ominous response: "Nothing." *You have to be kidding me*. I repeated the steps meticulously, and this time it went down. There seemed to be no trouble with it coming back up empty, so we quickly loaded it from the pile that had accumulated while it was in the hold below. Maybe we were over the hump, I thought. But no . . .

Bolstered by a successful round, I faithfully performed the sacred ritual like a duty-bound priest with the gate, door, shout, and button push, but to my frustration the offering had once again been rejected. Neptune was apparently not pleased with my amateur shipmate routine.

It was quickly becoming a personal challenge to get everything onboard that ship. Occasionally we managed multiple trips down the elevator shaft without interruption. But mostly it was just frustrating. I finally decided that this elevator was not going to win.

After we were finished loading, I took the steward aside. "Look, I have never worked on an elevator, but back home I fix nearly anything else. Could I see if I can fix your elevator?" I mean, it was just a freight elevator; it was not as though it was for people whose safety might be at risk.

"You're welcome to try," the steward replied, "but we had an elevator company look at it and they said it was too old. There was nothing they could do with it." As my wife would say, he might just as well have said "Sic 'em!" to me. That elevator was going to work before I got off that boat.

Although it was true that I had no experience troubleshooting elevators, I had lots of experience as an electrician, with electronics repair, and understanding mechanisms. I borrowed tools once again and pulled apart the safety switch mechanism for the security gate and door. Within minutes I had discovered the problem. Someone had disassembled the unit at one time and put some of the parts in backward. When I reassembled and tested the elevator it worked perfectly.

The steward was ecstatic—and hugged me. It meant so much to him personally, and to the crew, to have it working. After that my reputation quickly spread. Pretty soon there were other things people were asking me to look at, and I began to experience an inward struggle.

I had come to spend time with Jen, as well as hoping to see something of my birthplace. But as I saw pictures of the patients whose lives had been transformed by the procedures performed by hundreds of volunteer medical personnel working 12–14 hours day after day, year after year, I knew there was a more important reason for me to be there. Jen had to work during the day anyway, so I needed something to do. I yielded my rights to sightseeing and set to work.

Soon I was working on malfunctioning laundry equipment, and then the IT department needed some help. I embraced the fact that there had been a bigger picture for me to be part of in coming to this ship. It was about my place in Christ's kingdom, about being part of His body in ministering to the needs of those who were in turn ministering to the hopeless in the world, instead of just passing through like a tourist.

Sure, there was a tinge of disappointment that I had not been able to see some of the land in which I had been born, but that was nothing compared to the sense that I had served the Lord by helping many others. Besides, I probably wouldn't have been able to see the Loc Ness Monster anyway. But that was not the only unexpected trip I would make to England.

Fifteen years later someone paid the airfare for me to return to my birth country, this time with my wife. We traveled to Cambridge for a week and a half to see our daughter and son-in-law while he received his PhD—and I didn't have to fix a thing!

CHAPTER 23

What Was Spoken

"When the day of Pentecost had come, they were all together in one place. And suddenly there came from heaven a noise like a violent rushing wind, and it filled the whole house where they were sitting. And there appeared to them tongues as of fire distributing themselves, and they rested on each one of them. And they were all filled with the Holy Spirit and began to speak with other tongues, as the Spirit was giving them utterance.

"Now there were Jews living in Jerusalem, devout men from every nation under heaven. And when this sound occurred, the crowd came together, and were bewildered because each one of them was hearing them speak in his own language. They were amazed and astonished, saying, 'Why, are not all these who are speaking Galileans? And how is it that we each hear *them* in our own language to which we were born? Parthians and Medes and Elamites, and residents of Mesopotamia, Judea and Cappadocia, Pontus and Asia, Phrygia and Pamphylia, Egypt and the districts of Libya around Cyrene, and visitors from Rome, both Jews and proselytes, Cretans and Arabs—we hear them in our *own* tongues speaking of the mighty deeds of God.' And they all continued in amazement and great perplexity, saying to one another, 'What does this mean?'" Acts 2:1-12 (NASB)

Samuel (not his real name) got up and began to leave the meeting quickly. At the same time a man in the congregation also stood and met Samuel in the lobby of the church. Walking up to Samuel, the man began to talk to him in fluent Hebrew. Surprised, Samuel excitedly responded, "You know Hebrew!" The man just looked at Samuel and shook his head. He had no idea what he had said.

When Pentecost came after the resurrection of Jesus, an utterly astonishing sign to the Jewish nation took place. The disciples of Jesus suddenly were filled with the Holy Spirit and began speaking in languages they did not know, the common languages of a very wide range of countries around Israel. Not only were the disciples speaking in languages they did not know as the Holy Spirit empowered them, but they were specifically declaring the glories of God as they did so. Consequent to the sign and Peter's message, approximately three thousand Jews became disciples of Jesus and were baptized.

I had been a pastor for only a little over a year. One ministry area in which I had not had much education was that of counseling, so I was looking for opportunities that would begin to fill in gaps in my training. I signed up for an all-day seminar in Lansing, Michigan.

The speaker, Samuel, was both well prepared and entertaining, but something else seemed to catch my attention. Although he said nothing overtly, I got the distinct impression that he was a Christian. Our lunch was a catered meal at the meeting location, and I determined that I would try to eat with him. I made sure to get in line behind him as we got our food.

I introduced myself as we moved through the meal line and asked whether we could eat together, to which he agreed. When I asked if he was a Christian, he said he was, and I told him I would like to hear his salvation story. Samuel chuckled, and replied, "No, I don't think you would."

"No, really," I answered. "I love to hear how people have come to know the Lord." I talked him into it, and we sat down together at the table.

Samuel had been born and raised as a Jew. When a Jewish boy reaches the age of 13 he becomes a bar mitzvah, and the celebration of the event has the same name. Bar mitzvah is recognition that the responsibility for the boy's actions passes from the father to the child himself (bat mitzvah is the female version). Samuel learned Hebrew so he would be able to read from the Torah, the Jewish law comprised of the first five books of the Bible, at worship services, including his bar mitzvah, and to study the Old Testament in that language. But as a young man Samuel had grown away from interest in God before going on to college.

There Samuel was smitten with a beautiful young woman and did everything he could to get her to date him—to no avail. But he persisted, and finally she told him she would go out with him provided that he would go to church with her. He was torn by his desire for her and his reluctance to go to a Christian church, something he had never done before. In the end his romantic desires won out, and he agreed to attend. He had no idea what he was in for.

It turned out that the young woman attended a Pentecostal church, and when the pastor and the congregation got wound up it was more than Samuel could handle. When the service seemed to reach a fever pitch, Samuel decided to make an exit.

He got up to leave and headed for the door. At the same time another man in the congregation got up and met Samuel in the lobby as he was about to leave. Walking up to Samuel, he began to speak to him about God in fluent Hebrew. Totally caught off guard by someone he could relate to in the craziness, Samuel excitedly responded, "You know Hebrew!" to which the man just looked at him and shook his head no.

Samuel was no longer irritated by the zeal being displayed at the service. He was terrified. "God knows me!" reverberated in his head. The thought that God knew him personally—and was acquainted with his sins—overwhelmed his mind. Samuel ran into a room off the lobby and fell on his face in fear, crying out to God to save him. He received Christ as Savior that night.

I was skeptical, to say the least. I asked whether he himself was Pentecostal or charismatic? "No," Samuel responded.

"Do you speak in tongues?"

"No," he responded again. I had no reason to believe he had made up the story, there being no apparent motive for his having done so. I could say that I had never heard of such a thing, but that would be false.

In Acts, on the day of Pentecost, at that great gathering of Jews from all around the Mediterranean, the attendees heard the disciples miraculously proclaiming the greatness of God in their own known languages, and heard Peter warn them to flee from the wrath of God by putting their trust in Christ. Luke wrote that about three thousand Jews came to faith in Jesus as their Messiah that day.

I have to believe that Samuel experienced, in our day, the same manifestation of the Holy Spirit, and that it resulted in the call to a Jewish man to submit to the Jewish Messiah.

CHAPTER 24

Rain, Rain, Go Away

Jesus spent more than three years as a rabbi with a little group of disciples. It is true that they were part of a larger body of those referred to as disciples, but His primary focus was on the twelve, including Judas Iscariot, who would betray Him in the end.

At the end of that more than three years, just before going to the cross, Jesus told them that they would soon begin to pray in the authority of His name. In effect, it would be the same as if He were the one praying.

Jesus rebuked a storm, and it instantly subsided. If you consider what that meant, according to the laws of physics, the story becomes even more incredible. The wind and waves stopped, and conditions very quickly became calm. However, this is probably easier for me to believe than for most other people. In 1994 I did basically the same thing, praying in the name of Jesus, with a witness present: my oldest daughter, Jennifer.

I was a pastor at Westhaven Baptist Church in Port Huron, Michigan. We were going to be leaving the church to return to a Christian camping ministry near Alpena with which we had previously served. This resulted in my need to make a trip straight across the state to the Grand Junction area. The camp did not allow outdoor pets, so we had arranged to give our dog to my sister, who had a farm and lots of space for it. The dog was actually my daughter's, and she hated to part with it. I decided I would take her along to say goodbye when I dropped it off.

The air in Port Huron was damp, and clouds were thick as we loaded up the dog, dog house, and related paraphernalia into our Dodge Grand Caravan. You could smell rain in the air, and I expected it to start at any time. Mist started forming on the windshield before we reached the city limit.

As we headed west on the 230-mile trip, the rain steadily increased. By the time we reached Flint it was a constant shower, but by the time we got north of Lansing it was pouring proverbial cats and dogs, and I was concerned. Our minivan had a design problem. When it rained or snowed heavily the ignition system wiring would get wet, and the engine would start to miss. As hard as it was raining while driving onto the expressway, I knew this was inevitable. Suddenly I felt the first miss and knew what was coming, but I kept driving. I had no choice. I turned to my daughter and said, "Jen, start praying, because if this dies in this rain I will not be able to get it started again." We both prayed.

Then the intermittent miss became the total loss of one of the four cylinders. Soon I started to feel one of the last three start to miss. I sent up another urgent request: "Dear God, please just let me get off the expressway at Charlotte." The van was barely chugging up the ramp, and it was everything I could do to keep it going. The southbound exit at Charlotte is a downhill ramp to a stop sign because the expressway has an overpass. I knew what would happen at the stop sign, and the engine did die there in the rain. I tried several times, but it would not start.

As I sat there contemplating what to do, several verses came to my mind: "'Seek first the kingdom of God and his righteousness, and all these things [all else] will be added to you'" (Matthew 6:33). "'If you ask anything in my name, I will do it'" (John 14:14). "You do not have, because you do not ask. You ask and do not receive, because you ask wrongly, to spend it on your passions" (James 4:2–3).

"Elijah was a man with a nature like ours, and he prayed fervently that it might not rain, and for three years and six months it did not rain on the earth. Then he prayed again, and heaven gave rain, and the earth bore its fruit" (James 5:17–18). I knew how I needed to pray.

With the engine dead and the rain falling, I bowed my head and prayed: "Heavenly Father, to the best of my knowledge I am seeking first your kingdom and righteousness in my life. You have promised you will provide. I am told to ask and receive. Elijah was a man just like me, and he prayed it would not rain. I don't know a person here in Charlotte to help me, and I have got to get all this stuff to my sister. If it would be good and pleasing in your sight and in accordance with your plan and purpose in my life, I ask that it would stop raining long enough for me to get out and dry off the engine wiring. In Jesus' name, Amen." If I had not been there I would probably have had a hard time believing what happened next.

When I said "Amen," the rain stopped. It did not taper off slowly. It stopped. This was so abrupt that Jen and I stared at each other wide-eyed for a moment. The clouds opened up, exposing blue sky. This was the first time we had seen blue sky that morning. I reached under the driver's seat where I would usually put a rag and pulled out a full-sized rag towel I had stowed there instead. I popped the hood, got out, and quickly dried off all the spark plug wires and ignition parts. I closed the hood, got back in, and hit the key. The engine fired up, the clouds closed, and it started raining again. It then rained for the rest of the trip.

For the entire 230-mile trip there, the only time it did not rain was for exactly the length of time that I requested in prayer for it to stop.

Although most of the occasions have not been so dramatic, I have had rain stop after praying, or fail to come when forecast, at least a dozen times. On one more startling recent occasion I kept the radar image with date and time. Even if radar images had been an option for me at the time of this story, I doubt I could have gotten one accurate enough. The rain stopped for only about five minutes out of the whole trip across Michigan, and only where we were at that interstate ramp.

Perhaps the fact that it stopped raining for one time segment of the day is not persuasive enough.

As a part of the camp staff, one of my responsibilities was driving bus to take campers home and bring more loads of them to camp on the return trip. This was a 400-mile round trip that was not my favorite task. One thing that made it even less enjoyable was doing it in the rain. Not only did getting soaked make you feel uncomfortable, but moisture from the rain-soaked kids would accumulate on windows, making visibility difficult at best on occasions.

We made stops at Bay City, Flint, and Lansing, with two rest stops as well along the I-75/69 route. At each the drivers would have to get off the buses to help unload luggage from our semi-trailer on the way downstate.

On one particular trip down it was starting to sprinkle before we left camp, and my mood was pessimistic about the possibility for rain throughout the whole trip. Our first stop would be Bay City, a little over an hour away, and as we drove I remembered the occasion of praying that the rain would stop as we had driven across the state a couple of years earlier. I thought it couldn't hurt to try and decided that if it was raining when we got to Bay City I would ask for it to stop. It was, and I did. It rained all the way to the department store parking lot where we would drop off kids, but as the tires of my bus reached the entrance of the large parking lot the rain began to taper off. By the time we swung around behind the store and reached our destination on the far side of the parking lot—about a minute—the rain had stopped.

"Wow!" I thought to myself, but I didn't say anything to any of the other drivers. We got the kids and the baggage off, and as we began to roll it started raining again. At the rest stop the same thing happened, and then again at Flint and at the last rest stop. It would stop raining as we arrived and start again as we left. But it was raining harder as we came within a few miles of our final stop at the old Lansing Mall on the northwest side of the city. The radio chatter of our drivers started to pick up that we were "going to get wet this time."

By now I couldn't restrain myself. I got on the radio and said, "No, we won't. At every stop on this trip I have prayed that it would stop raining so we would not get soaked. I have asked it again for Lansing." Again, it was a very large parking area, and by the time our busses stopped the rain had as well.

I thought that a storm "responding" to prayer in a contemporary setting was unusual, but a young man who was the son of an itinerant minister came up to me after I had shared my story of taking our dog across the state. He told me of two occasions from his own life when the same thing had happened.

"When I was in first grade, my dad took me out west to Nebraska, where he had been a rural missionary. Real cowboy country. On the way out there, we hit a rainstorm. It was the middle of nowhere in some flat part of America. The rain kept getting heavier and heavier until it sounded like thunder in our Astro minivan. My dad could no longer see out the window, so we stopped along the side of the road. I was scared but trying not to show it. So we prayed. As a father, I know now how much faith it takes to pray for specifics with your children. You feel as though there's a risk. If the prayer isn't answered in the affirmative, how will your child process the outcome? So now, when I look back and think that my dad actually prayed for the rain to stop, I'm even more amazed at his faith. We prayed together in that little van, and the rain stopped instantly. There was no question that God turned the rain off. This was one of my earliest memories of seeing God revealed in a tangible way."

He had been a teenager when the second instance occurred.

"Years later, I was in high school, and my dad took a group of us high schoolers from church to North Dakota to do a vacation Bible school for a house church there. After a week of preparation, canvasing the neighborhood and setting up outside games, we got another rainstorm. Sideways rain is a thing in North Dakota. No one was going to come unless the rain stopped. I can't remember whose idea it was, but we prayed for the rain to stop. The very moment we said 'Amen,' the rain stopped and we had our VBS. This had a huge impact on us."

One could be forgiven for reasoning that these were simply stories that the teenager had made up, trying to impress me after hearing my own testimony, . . . except for two factors. First, I knew the young man well, and I knew he would not lie to me. Second, I knew that my including accounts I had not been party to in this book could easily be dismissed by skeptical readers. So, while writing this chapter I phoned the young man's father, whom I will call Robert in order to avoid endangering the son. I asked him to recount the stories in his own words. Everything the teenager had told me was true. But Robert added even more impressive details to the two stories.

The storm in the southwest corner of Nebraska, on what is now Highway 83 between North Platte and McCook, almost seventy miles to the south, produced rain so heavy it was impossible to see to drive. The windshield wipers were useless. Robert quickly pulled the minivan to the side of the road and parked. Dale didn't want his dad to think he was frightened, but in truth both of them were scared. What scared Robert the most was knowing that if he couldn't see to drive, neither could anyone else. "You couldn't even see the lights of other vehicles," he said. He was afraid someone might be driving blind and run into them.

Robert recalled the fear of the disciples during the storm on the Sea of Galilee, and prayed loudly enough for his son to hear him over the roar of the rain. "Lord, you rebuked the wind and the waves. Would you stop this rain?" When he said "Amen," the torrential downpour stopped. That was amazing enough. But then, looking out the windows, Robert realized it had stopped raining only where they were. All around them he could see that it was still pouring.

The storm in North Dakota also occurred just as Dale had told me. Robert and his wife were in charge of ministry to a large youth group. The summer in question she took half the youth group to Alaska on a missions trip, and Robert took the other half to North Dakota. A local missionary with the Rural Home Missionary Association asked for a group to come to survey a small town and conduct a VBS. It all happened just as Dale had recounted the incident to me.

His father added that they had gotten permission to use an abandoned greenhouse as a meeting place and had a great deal of work to do to make it usable. They got it all cleared out and set up some game areas outside. The youth group canvased the entire small town and invited many to come. But early on the morning of the scheduled day heavy wind and rain set in. They prayed, some as a group and a few individuals on their own, and when they were done the rain stopped, the sun and wind dried out the area, and the VBS was held as planned.

If these accounts aren't impressive enough on their own, I cannot help but marvel at an even more detailed story from the life of Watchman Nee, a Chinese Christian evangelist during the 1950s–70s, as recorded by Angus Kinnear, in *Against the Tide*. As a consequence, not of Nee's *canceling* but of his *causing* a torrential rainstorm from a sunny sky, a local pagan deity was dethroned in a village that had been completely resistant to the gospel. Astonished, the inhabitants turned to the one true God who had made the impossible happen.

After these and other stories like them, I am convinced that events of this nature are far more common manifestations of the reality and power of God than anyone realizes. This being the case, there is one puzzling question: Why don't we hear about them?

My opinion is that this is the case for one simple reason: we consider our reputations more important than His. The next chapter addresses that problem.

CHAPTER 25

Quench Not

"**Y**ou aren't here to take pictures . . ." I was about to get one of the most unusual ministry opportunities from the Lord I have ever had. But taking it meant putting my pride on the shelf.

While I was a self-supporting missionary in Christian camping, I decided I needed to come up with a way to generate a little more income in my spare time. The apostle Paul had done tent making to help support his ministry. The same kind of freelance photography I had done for a number of years before I had gone to Bible school seemed like it could work for me to fit into the cracks in my schedule. It would also mean I could be more engaged with our community, and allowed me to accumulate camera equipment I was able to use in our ministry at the same time.

I ended up becoming a "stringer" for our local paper, the *Oscoda County Herald*; the regional *Bay City Times*; and their magazine, *True North*. I shot lots of sports and feature photos and wrote stories for a few years and really enjoyed it. My artistic talents had been dormant for a while, and it felt good to utilize them again.

On October 18, 2007, I needed to cover girls' volleyball home games at both of our local schools, Mio and Fairview. Time was always tight when I had to cover both teams on their home courts in the same evening, and compounding the stress of one particular such instance was a powerful storm that was coming in across the county, not the sort of conditions in which I wanted to be hauling around my expensive camera equipment. Maybe I could get done early and beat the storm.

I lived only five minutes from Fairview, so I stopped there and shot until I knew I had enough pics for a story I could get from the coach on the phone later. Then I headed to Mio, another fifteen minutes away. The storm was building a few miles to the west, and the lightning was pretty ominous. But it wasn't thunder I heard as I grabbed my two bags of equipment and climbed out of my car in the high school parking lot.

"You aren't here to take pictures. You are here to cheerlead." *What on earth?* I was there as a reporter and photographer. I had work to do. I was used to the Lord speaking to me about things related to ministry, but *cheerleading*? I was about to get a new perspective on what ministry to kids could look like.

The Mio Lady Thunderbolts were playing the Lady Tigers of Hillman, the Northstar League-leading team, and Mio was getting pummeled. But what really grabbed my attention was that the gym was more like a tomb than a sporting venue. Aside from the squeaking of tennis shoes, the thump of the ball, and official whistles, you wouldn't know anyone beside the teams was there.

That the Mio girls were getting beaten was not surprising. Hillman was good, really good, and probably everyone in the stands expected them to win. But what was surprising was how poorly Mio was playing. They were a good team too, but their hearts weren't in it; it was as though they had simply resigned themselves to the inevitable. I suddenly realized the significance of what I had heard as I had gotten out of the car. I knew what I needed to do.

I shot pics as quickly as I could to make sure I had something for the paper and then put away my camera gear. I was across the gym from the stands and couldn't help but anticipate what people were going to think. But I ignored the crowd because their presence really didn't matter. Mio had lost the first game 5-25. I was going to try to make sure the score wasn't close to that in the second.

As a troubled teen myself, from the ages of 16-18 my single most recurring thought was that of killing myself. I wasn't smart, popular, athletic, tough, or anything else that seemed to matter in that age group. I was one thing, though: hopeless.

In elementary school I remember always being the last one picked for a team activity. Even at that age it meant a lot to be good at sports. When I was 16 I remember looking up into a starry sky one night and saying to myself, *If I ever find anything that gives meaning to life for a teenager, that is what I will give my life to.* It didn't occur to me that Someone might be listening.

From the time I was saved in 1979, I was continuously involved at some level or other in ministry to kids. This covered the spectrum from very young children through high schoolers. I had the opportunity to minister to a few thousand kids over the course of my ministry years, especially in Christian camping. I had a heart for them regardless of whether or not they were directly under my care, and I always tried to give them hope and encouragement. At that point the kids in the gym were going to get something from me none of us expected.

At every point during the second game I cheered—er, screamed—encouragement for the Mio girls at the top of my voice. That wasn't exactly kosher, since a reporter isn't supposed to take sides, but I really didn't care. If they missed a shot, I shouted, "It's okay—you can do it! You'll get it next time!" If they got the point or save I was a lunatic of praise: "Great shot! Great save! Great job!" At first the players just looked at me, which was fine because the people in the stands were staring at the madman across the gym too. And then something happened.

The girls started to believe in themselves.

Suddenly they were diving and digging to make impossible saves. They were running full tilt off court to return balls deflected by team members, running into the stands if they had to. This was what I knew they were capable of. By the end of the second game, the score was 25-20, with Mio on top.

The Lady Bolts had just taken a "knockdown, drag out" game from the league-leading Tigers. They came off the court jumping and squealing with joy, and Hillman wondered what had just happened. But there wasn't to be a fairy tale ending—the Bolts ended up losing each of the next two games 15-20 to the Tigers. The Bolts were exhausted by the end, but there was no shame in the loss. The girls knew they had played their best and made Hillman work hard for every point of the last two games. The referees later told me that this was the best volleyball they had seen all season.

What if I had refused my "assignment" for the evening? What if I had been more concerned about protocol than about kids on a court in front of the hometown crowd? What if my pride had been more important to me than their self-confidence and I was afraid of looking like a crazy man in front of the fans? I could have said no, but I am so glad I didn't. And by the way, once I began acting like a fanatic, others started cheering too.

Fear of embarrassment may be the single biggest hindrance to ministry there is. When we refuse or resist the prompting of the Holy Spirit, it is called quenching the Spirit.

People rank the fear of public speaking above that of death! I never told the team that I had become a cheerleader that night because the Lord had asked me to. I wish I had. Would it have made any difference to them? Maybe not. But maybe someone might have been encouraged to seek the Lord because of it.

How many of us don't engage others in the name of the Lord because we are afraid to share our testimony, even if we know how? How often do we avoid speaking to others who are suffering because we fear not having answers to the tough questions and broken hearts? How often do we choose not to associate with those whose lives are a wreck, like the woman at the well, or Mary Magdalene, or the demoniac of Gadara, because of what people may think of us?

"You're here to cheerlead . . ." My becoming a cheerleader at a volleyball game didn't change the world. *Why would God care about something like that? Why would he ask me to risk looking like an idiot?* Because he cares about people, whether or not they love him, and I was available to minister to the need of their hearts.

There are times the Holy Spirit may ask us to be available to minister in ways that seem odd, perhaps even embarrassing. Hosea was asked to marry a prostitute, and take her back after she had been unfaithful as a picture of God's relationship to unfaithful Israel. Isaiah was asked to walk half naked and barefoot for three years as a warning to Egypt and Cush. Peter was asked three times to kill and eat unclean food, a very offensive request for a devout Jew, but important to revealing God's change of relationship with Gentiles.

Sometimes God asks his servants to go to unusual or even extreme lengths because he cares about people, whether they love him or not. I was available to minister to the need of the hearts of the girls on that team, even if I did seem crazy doing it.

I have no regrets that I obeyed, but I sure would have if I had quenched the Spirit.

CHAPTER 26

Setting Captives Free

"**S**teve, Steve! You aren't going to believe what happened!" I got a sinking feeling in my stomach as the young man ran toward me. Being discipled in dealing with spiritual powers of darkness taught me to expect resistance when opposing them. I had just taken them on to set a young boy free from their grip.

My involvement with occult practices prior to becoming a disciple of Jesus opened the door for demonic influence in my life, perhaps in the same sense as for Mary Magdalene, from whom Jesus drove out seven demons. We really don't know any details about how they gained control, or what Jesus did to deal with them. His technique seemed to vary from case to case. Saying that, I can guess what some are thinking.

Sometimes, when demonic control is mentioned in a person's life, visions of scenes from *The Exorcist* come to mind. In reality, the Greek term *daimonidzomai*, rendered in the New Testament as "demon possessed," is very much like the contemporary English word "sick" in its range of meaning. The expression "I'm sick" could represent anything from having a cold to having terminal cancer. In the same way, people with demonic influence in their lives can have manifestations that run from barely noticeable to totally out-of-control behavior.

The summer of 1985 I was an activities programmer at Camp

Barakel. I joined the summer staff with this background awareness of the demonic issue, from my own life and from those of others as well. I read in the Gospels about how common it was to deal with dark spiritual influences as a key to spiritual freedom, and this lined up with my own experience. In my case the manifestation was essentially unnoticeable.

I was aware of the tendency for demons to manifest when preaching takes place, or in the Lord's presence, as noted in the Gospels. I had been at camp for a winter teen retreat before we joined the summer staff, when a demon had to be dealt with in one of the teenagers after an evening chapel service. I expected that the same thing might happen during my time as a part of the summer crew. So I wasn't surprised when one of the guy counselors came to me a few weeks into the camp schedule. I will call the counselor George, and his camper Joey.

"Steve, I don't know what to do!" he blurted in frustration. "One of the boys in my 'tribe' (which is what we called each counselor/camper group) reacts every time we do something spiritual. Praying for a meal, doing morning devotions, going to chapel—all of it sets him off. I haven't been able to listen to one message in chapel because I am so busy trying to keep Joey under control."

I had talked to the camp director, Roger Williams, about my occult involvement prior to salvation, as well as about my training on how to deal with demons by a brother in Christ, Brett Strong. I wanted to make myself available to work with any such situations that might come up, but I also recognized a concern many Christians have about demonic confrontation. I promised I would go to our camp chaplain, Fred Moore, if I felt there was a need to deal with a demonic influence in one of the campers.

Fred was one of the most humble, quiet servants of God I had ever met. He was a delight to be around and talk to about the things of the Lord. After discussing with him what was happening with Joey, he agreed that this sounded like it might be demonic in nature, and I had his blessing to proceed. I talked to George and let him know I would like to come to pray with his tribe before he held morning devotions the next day.

The vast majority of situations dealing with demons are nothing at all like what you see in movies. Only a very small number of instances involve threatening behavior by those under demonic influence. There are adequate measures which can subdue the powers of darkness. There won't be room in this book for specifics; for more information on that subject I highly recommend the books on spiritual warfare by Neil Anderson.

I met George and his boys in the morning and told them I was there to pray with them before George led them in studying their verse for the day.

We all bowed our heads, and I took authority over any wicked spirits that might be present. I prayed that any demons would be silenced so they could not interfere with any of the boys, preventing them from hearing, understanding, or responding to the gospel. This is very important because of one principle clearly taught by the Lord in Matthew 13, Mark 4, and Luke 8, in the parable of the sower. Jesus spoke of birds stealing the seeds of the sower along the path: "'Now the parable is this: The seed is the word of God. The ones along the path are those who have heard; then the devil comes and takes away the word from their hearts, so that they may not believe and be saved'" (Luke 8:11–12).

The seeds represent teaching of the Word of God, and the birds represent the work of accusing spirits (Greek *diabolos*) taking those words away from those who did not understand and receive the teaching. Soil represents the hearts of people, while the path represents soil trodden down. One of the most significant reasons people reject the teaching of the kingdom of God is that their hearts have been made hard by the offenses of people against them. Accusing spirits keep those offenses in the forefront of a person's mind and wipe out the words of the kingdom so they have no effect.

I am guessing that the average reader might have little to no understanding of what that kind of prayer might be like. But there was no shouting, no calling out of Joey or embarrassing him in any way. I realize that a few cases in Scripture record that Jesus used a loud voice in dealing with demons, but that was not necessary in our situation, and seldom is.

Toward the end of my prayer I paused to see whether there was a reaction from Joey, but none was evident. In fact, after George's description I was really surprised by how quiet he was. I finished praying and headed up to prepare for flag raising, leaving George with his tribe.

Maybe 15 minutes later, George came flying over the top of the rise from where they had been for devotions behind the nurse's station. "Steve! Steve! You aren't going to believe what happened!" At this point I had visions of Joey going nuts after I left, and my summer experience blowing up in my face. "What?" I asked, more than a little concerned at what he might say.

"I gave a gospel invitation at the end of devos, and Joey responded. He asked Jesus to be his Savior!" George was out of breath. I was excited—and Joey was changed. The rest of that week George didn't have another incident with him during prayers or chapels. His behavior bore witness that he had indeed received salvation and that the powers of darkness were no longer in control in his life.

A number of years later I ran into George, who had since become a pastor and speaker. I was excited to see him and laughed as I told him how much "mileage" I had gotten out of that story. I had used it to teach others about the need to deal with demonic influences, particularly when presenting the gospel to someone who is resistant to it.

The smile slowly left George's face. He looked at me and lowered his voice. "I have never told anyone that story." I was dumbfounded.

"Why?" I asked.

"Because I was afraid of how people would react, what they would say," came the reply. I could hardly believe it, and to be honest it just made me sad. There is little wonder at disbelief of the supernatural reality of God when we refuse to speak of those things around others.

It is a travesty, and it robs God of the glory He deserves, when we are afraid to tell others of the ways in which He supernaturally manifests His presence and power. We are stealing the heritage of the children of God when we are ashamed to talk openly about His victory over the enemy of our souls. Let us not be ashamed to declare the reality of God's intervention, power, and provision in our lives.

The stones of remembrance are crucial as evidence of the reality of God's provision, direction, protection, indeed his intervention in the lives of people. Those events are the pillar we can pass on to those who follow us on our journeys.

I am fully convinced one factor has contributed significantly to the exodus of young people from churches to the "nones" category. It is lack of contemporary evidence of God at work in our day.

Every Christian should have a pillar of stones to share with others.

CHAPTER 27

Falling

The tires of the ambulance crunched to a stop at the edge of the highway. The paramedic did a quick assessment of vitals and turned to the driver: "We have to get to the hospital NOW!" The driver hit the gas pedal, and the ambulance tore off toward the regional medical center, with a terrified wife trying to keep up in her car behind them.

A couple of hours earlier it had been a routine, beautiful northern Michigan morning at a regional track meet for a half dozen rural high school teams. As a writer/photographer for both a local and a regional newspaper, I was there to cover the meet.

I decided to take my daughter, Sarah, along for the shoot. Only a teenager, she was quickly distinguishing herself as a talented photojournalist. I would need her help to cover as many events as possible. This was more than just a gathering of wannabe high school track heroes. There was genuine state-level talent scattered throughout the crowd, and record setting was far from being out of the question in several of the competitions.

We had already shot pole vault and high jump events, and I decided we should shoot the discus throw together, something Sarah had never covered before. Rather than standing behind the thrower, where it would be extremely difficult to get a good shot, we walked out along the throwing lane, but stayed out of it 15 feet or so to the left for safety. We were far enough downrange that even if a throw was off we could easily step out of the way.

As we were setting up long lenses to capture the throwers, I noticed that the front element of Sarah's lens was dirty. "Oh, you don't want to shoot with that. Let me clean it for you," I offered. Sarah handed me her camera and lens, and I reached around to my camera bag for my lens-cleaning pen.

It was his first competition. The young high schooler had just taken up discus, and he had never thrown one in an actual track meet. Some of his schoolmates were behind the backstop watching, and that made him nervous enough. He certainly didn't want to look foolish. What was worse were the two newspaper photographers with the big cameras off to his left. He was only throwing a hard rubber practice discus weighing about three-and-a-half pounds, but the reporters didn't need to know that.

He felt awkward as he wound up for the throw, but soon it was in its arc. It wouldn't come near a record mark for distance, but it was about to do something remarkable, inexplicable, that would leave an indelible mark on someone who was least expecting it.

The discus abruptly turned to its left, out of the throwing lane, an oddity noticed by the teens behind the backstop. In fact, a discus under normal circumstances can't do what that one did that morning.

The young high schooler and his classmates quickly calculated the trajectory in their minds and watched in horror as the discus headed straight for the photographers who were intent on cleaning a camera lens. The teens screamed a warning to the twosome, but with all the noise of ongoing contests and cheering teams the warning was swallowed up. They never saw it coming.

Falling. Why was I falling? And why did my face hurt?

Suddenly everything was black, and I felt myself crashing straight backward, like a northern white pine severed from its stump. I knew I was going down, but there was nothing I could do to stop myself. I just braced for the impact.

With her back to the thrower, the spinning disk just cleared Sarah's head and shoulder and struck me squarely in the middle of my lower jaw. Even though I had never been in a boxing ring, I could now say I knew what it felt like to get *KO*d. Three EMTs in the crowd as spectators were on the run before I even hit the ground.

The high schooler came unglued. His first throw in a high school competition, and he had just killed someone. At least, from all appearances, that was what he thought. A sheriff's deputy whisked him off to a school bus to calm him down while the EMTs worked on me, and a crowd gathered around them.

Now hysterical, Sarah had been only inches from me as the discus hit me in the face. In an instant everything was chaos as the EMTs and crowd swarmed us. Blood was gushing from my mouth. A CT scan at the regional medical center in West Branch later that day would reveal that my jaw was split cleanly in two in the exact center, and that a big chunk of the left side was snapped loose, with the teeth still in it.

Sobbing uncontrollably, Sarah tried to call her mother, who at first couldn't tell whether she was laughing or crying. Finally, Sarah managed to get out, "It's dad—come quickly." Audrey could not ever remember having driven anywhere as fast as she covered the five miles to town.

I felt the teeth in my mouth, but I had to keep spitting out blood. I was afraid my teeth might get lost in the mess. With my jaw split in two and a big piece broken off, it took several attempts to get the EMTs to understand that I wondered whether they saw my teeth in the pool of blood. They did not. Up to that moment I had no fear about what was happening—only confusion as to what had caused the situation. But fear was about to make an appearance on the scene.

I had been trained as a first responder, so I understood what they were doing to help me, and I complied. Then suddenly, as they slowly rotated my head and neck upright to immobilize them, terror struck. I realized their training was about to kill me. I began to drown in my own blood.

Unable to breathe because of the blood, and unable to speak because of the facial damage, I could only seize their hands and wrench them loose to let me get my face to the side, mouth emptied, and gasp for air. One of the local coaches later told me, "I worked my way through the crowd to see who was injured, but you had lost so much blood any skin that wasn't covered in red was as gray as a sweatshirt. I didn't know who you were."

Although EMTs were there, they were only spectators, so there was no emergency kit immediately available to stop the blood flow. A friend of mine, Pete (who could not stand the sight of blood) was at my side and pulled his shirt off for them to use.

After a few minutes I realized I had been panicked the whole time and had to relax or I would increase the likelihood of shock setting in. I said a prayer in my mind, trusting God for whatever might happen and forcing myself to relax.

Pete saw one of the EMTs reacting strongly. "What's wrong?" he asked.

The EMT just looked at him. "What usually happens is: they turn gray, they relax, and then they die." I was totally unaware that I had just nearly caused them to have cardiac arrests.

Because of cell tower overlap the 911 call for the ambulance had gone to the wrong county dispatch center, but the dispatcher quickly figured out what had happened and contacted the local Oscoda ~~Franklin~~ County EMS. After what seemed like an eternity the EMS crew arrived, and we headed out on the 40-mile drive to the regional medical center in West Branch. En route I started to lose consciousness, prompting the stop along the highway.

Audrey, now following them, panicked when they pulled off the road. *What on earth!? This can't be good.* When they took off at a high speed her own heart rate increased in keeping with the speedometer.

The CT scan revealed that the injury exceeded their capabilities, and the nearest maxillofacial surgeon was over a hundred miles away. Two more friends joined us at West Branch and drove Audrey and me to Flint, where I would wait over twenty hours to see the surgeon. Car crash victims kept bumping me down the list.

It was a scene out of the TV show *ER*. Staff was laughing, joking, . . . and ordering pizza. Knife and gunshot wounds kept coming in. Once a room finally opened up for me, they got me on morphine, which made me loopy on top of everything else. In the middle of the night a young doctor came to my bedside and introduced himself. "I'm on your surgical team. I was in track in college, and I was just curious to see what someone looks like after being hit in the face by a discus." Great! Now I was part of the *Late Show* entertainment . . .

Ultimately Humpty Dumpty was successfully put back together and my jaw wired shut for a month. But as my wife noted, this didn't stop me from talking. Everything I ate had to go through a blender, including a cheeseburger and pizza. It was interesting how no one wanted to eat around me.

When a charismatic sister in Christ in our community, Patricia, heard that morning of the accident she started praying for me. She later told me something, a missing puzzle piece, that explained why a discus had defied the laws of physics, even though she was totally unaware of the details of the accident.

She said that as she prayed for me the Lord revealed to her that Satan had tried to kill me but that God had not allowed it. To be honest, although I am aware of the warfare of Satan against believers, I am not one who suspects a demon in every doorknob. So, with no way to verify such a statement, I was skeptical about that part. Then a week later I saw the same kids at another track meet, and they told me what they had seen the discus do. A discus does not—

cannot—turn like that one did. There was no physical explanation for how it had behaved, but now there was a possible spiritual one.

People become "nones" for different reasons. But one of the most common is the experience of tragedy—either their own or someone else's. People feel as though God has abandoned His responsibility when He is needed most. I suggest that the problem is not with God but with our perception of Him.

One of the most relevant explanations of this problem of perception may be found in the book of Job. This devoted follower of God, diligent businessman, committed father, and liberal philanthropist lost nearly everything, including his health. His wife, however, lost the one thing he did not—hope. After years of enjoying the blessing of God, this was too much for her, and she became a "none." Job remained loyal to Yahweh, but his wife did her best to get him to abandon God: "Curse God and die!" she cried in her despair.

What frustrates, and in some cases infuriates, people almost more than anything else about God is that oftentimes He does not act in the way they expect Him to. We want to create God in our own image. When He doesn't fit into our box, we either look for a bigger box or reject God.

In Satan's challenge of God in Job, he was granted control, not only of people but even of nature in order to afflict Job and destroy his family. I knew Satan could influence people, but had he been able to change the direction of the discus at the track meet with a gust of wind, much as he had brought about the whirlwind that destroyed Job's house?

In the case of Job's tragedy, his wife gave up. What good was it to be faithful to a god you couldn't trust to provide continuous, dependable benefits? The man of God, however, didn't give up, and he even tried to reason her back. "But he said to her, 'You speak as one of the foolish women would speak. Shall we receive good from God, and shall we not receive evil?' In all this Job did not sin with his lips" (Job 2:10).

Job acknowledged the sovereignty of God in both good and evil events in life. He just wanted to correct Him. "I don't deserve this!" was the chant he kept repeating to himself and to those who had come to comfort their suffering friend. If he could just argue his case before God he could prove it. Job would eventually get the opportunity, . . . and regret it.

What neither Job nor his wife knew was that his misfortunes were a series of direct attacks on them and their family in order to break him. Although there had been a "hedge" of protection around them for years because of Job's faithfulness, it had been withdrawn so that God's greater purpose could be served.

God set boundaries that their spiritual enemies could not cross—until He allowed it. Even then Satan could go only so far and no farther. What the two of them experienced meant sorrow for them but was for the benefit of the sons of God who would follow in their footsteps. No other book of the Bible so clearly defines the opposition of Satan to the kingdom of God, nor the protection of God on our behalf. Their experience of suffering was meant to help us understand this dimension of the spiritual realm in a way mere theory could never do.

Does God have that right? Is it simply His choice whether to allow, or even cause, circumstances of difficulty, pain, and loss when He deems it necessary? Scripture teaches that it is, and Yahweh Himself experienced that suffering in the rejection and death of Jesus on the cross.

It is this lack of perspective that pushes many into the category of "nones."

Was Patricia right? Did Satan try to kill me that morning? I have no way to prove or disprove this theory, but there seems to be no other plausible explanation for what the discus did. There was no wind that day to change its direction. She claimed that God prevented a fatal attack. If He did, why did He allow the discus to hit me in the face? Does God have the "right" to make that kind of decision?

Consider the partial grocery list of afflictions that the apostle Paul suffered for the sake of Christ, as recorded in 2 Corinthians 11:24–27:

> "Five times I received at the hands of the Jews the forty lashes less one. Three times I was beaten with rods. Once I was stoned. Three times I was shipwrecked; a night and a day I was adrift at sea; on frequent journeys, in danger from rivers, danger from robbers, danger from my own people, danger from Gentiles, danger in the city, danger in the wilderness, danger at sea, danger from false brothers; in toil and hardship, through many a sleepless night, in hunger and thirst, often without food, in cold and exposure."

He even wrote in chapter 12:7 of a thorn in the flesh as a direct attack of Satan. Yes, God has the right, and in light of what Paul and Job faced, I got off pretty light if that was all Satan was allowed to do to me.

Revelation 12:17 tells us that Satan, the great dragon, was furious that he missed his opportunity to put an end to Jesus, and that he went off to make war against his followers. We should take that seriously and do what we must do to remain under the protection of God and deliver others from Satan's destructive control.

CHAPTER 28

Mountaintop Experiences

I sat in my office, not wanting to allow myself to be discouraged. But there was no getting around the fact that my decision had brought the project I was managing to what appeared to be a dead end. Was I wrong? Had I gone too far wanting to walk by faith, and was I jeopardizing the project by being stubborn?

In April of 2008 we moved to Ozark, Arkansas, to be a short-term part of the ministry of Youth With A Mission. Jim Nizza and the crew had planted a new campus on Manitou Mountain, which comes from a native American word meaning "mountain of God."

Jim had invited me to come to their campus for a big project that required a live-in project manager. The property had a cafetorium, a combination dining and meeting building, in very bad condition. He needed someone to oversee the renovation project that would end up requiring 18 months of supervision for the first phase.

The project would be done as the money and help were supplied. I was used to that philosophy from my previous experience as part of the year 'round Christian camp ministry. YWAM uses large numbers of volunteers to do the organization's facility work, and one such group on which they rely heavily is called Mission Builders. Its members are volunteers who come with skills and tools, or sometimes with just a willing heart and hands. Working with volunteers like that can be a huge blessing—or a nightmare for a project coordinator.

I wanted to do more than repair a building. I wanted to compile a list of God stories throughout the course of the project, instances in which God had demonstrated His involvement in what we were doing. In some cases that might put us in the difficult situation of waiting on God to act or answer a prayer, but Jim and I agreed that this was what we both wanted.

That supernatural intervention was consistent with the roots of Christian ministry on the mountain. The following is borrowed from the website of the YWAM Ozarks:

"Our presence on Manitou Mountain in Ozark is rooted in an event in 1946. That year, Rev. A. H. Levin traveled from Wisconsin to his church's mission outreach in Arkansas. While in the area, he recalled being asked to run a Bible College in Ozark years earlier. He inquired about it out of curiosity and learned it was shut down. 'But there is a place that would be perfect for a Bible College,' insisted a local pastor. Rev. Levin had no interest in starting a school, but this pastor was so persistent that he finally went along.

"He was taken up the winding road to the top of Manitou Mountain and while looking around someone said, 'This is the place for a Bible School.' Rev. Levin turned to see who had spoken but no one was there. It was a sovereign call of God. The property, including a gorgeous lodge and some smaller buildings, was his in three weeks—82 acres for $7000. In less than a year Ozark Bible Institute was incorporated. Rev. Levin was 'Grandpa' to Barb Nizza, present YWAM Ozarks director."

I was excited to be even a temporary part of a campus with that kind of spiritual heritage, and we were about to see God's hand in it in no less dramatic fashion carrying on the same kind of evidence of His involvement.

We gutted the kitchen and dining room, literally tearing off everything down to the studs in the walls, stripping the floors to bare concrete, and removing a huge commercial stove, vent hood, and twenty-foot stainless steel counter and storage shelf unit. Seeing that there had been two painted floor coverings lasting about ten years each, and then a thin tiled floor over those that had lasted a little over ten years before falling apart, created a dilemma for me. We were going to put a huge amount of work and money into the building. Clearing the kitchen area made me realize that potentially in ten years they could need to replace the floor yet again if we followed the previous methods. I wanted to make sure that did not happen.

As I explored flooring options I realized that the only one guaranteed to last longer in a commercial kitchen setting without being easily chipped or damaged would be a porcelain tile floor. But porcelain tiles are extremely expensive, costing in some cases well over five dollars for one square-foot tile. With an entire building to re-floor, there would be no money in the project to cover this unexpected huge cost for four thousand square feet.

As it turned out, this was exactly the scenario I had originally hoped would present itself—a big need that would allow God to display his ability to hear and answer prayer. But it also produced a struggle to know how to deal with everything else that needed to happen as well. As the project coordinator my responsibility was to keep things moving, with volunteers coming in to help on a fairly regular basis.

We worked on every small job that could be accomplished, up to the point of putting down flooring, and kept looking for God to provide. But the list finally ran out, and no big donations had come in to cover the extra we would need. I sat in my office one morning facing the fact that something had to happen immediately. Looking across the property at the now empty building, I felt myself to be between that proverbial rock and a hard place. I had new empathy for King Saul, who saw his people losing heart in 1 Samuel 13 and "forced himself" to violate protocol in the matter of offering a sacrifice, ultimately thereby losing his place of leadership.

I bowed my head and spoke to the Lord about the situation, reminding Him of my desire to see Him prove Himself able to meet our needs. I talked about my desire to do work on the building that would last for many years to come, and about the need for flooring that we could not afford. "We have done everything we can before putting floor down. We have to hear from you now. What shall I do?"

I sat in my office that morning working on project plans, since I had no work crews on the property. A phone call came in a couple of hours later. It was Jim, telling me that another volunteer was on the outside line wanting to set up a time to come help with the renovation. I hate to admit that at that moment I was not encouraged by having to coordinate more volunteer help when I had no idea when we would be able to continue working. Our backs were to the wall until God would provide somehow. It is a great philosophy to live by personally, but not so much fun or practical when you are the one everyone else is waiting on. But I told Jim I would take the call.

We introduced ourselves briefly, and I took the usual notes: name, phone number, prospective dates, and so forth. In this case the caller and a friend wanted to come together and stay in their own RV. "What kinds of skills do you have?" I asked. I was used to responses ranging from some to none.

"Well," he replied, "I can do a little bit of everything, but my friend is really good at laying floor." I swear, outside of Jim and myself, no one knew the situation we were facing except the Lord, and I had just talked to Him about it before the call came in.

"It's interesting that you called," I said, trying to hide the excitement that was starting to build. "We are at a point in our project where we have to lay flooring before we can do anything else."

"What is it you want to put down?" he asked.

"Well, what we want to install is a high-grade porcelain tile floor, but we don't have the money for that," I replied.

"No kidding!" he said. "Down the road from me is a surplus building supply company that is going out of business. They have pallets of porcelain tile they are selling for five dollars a box. But I think I might be able to talk them down to two or three dollars a box. How much do you need, and what color?" This alone was astonishing, because anything high quality I had seen had been selling for five dollars or more per tile, and there were normally ten or more tiles to a box.

I was so excited at this point that I indicated we would even settle for puce if we could get porcelain tile for that price. He gave me some options and checked to see whether they had the required quantity. We ended up with a beautiful blue gray tile that covered all of the areasr.

The total price for the tile? Three hundred dollars. The whole experience to get a God story? Priceless. The guy and his buddy ended up donating their time to come, get the installation underway, and teach us how to do the rest, and even paid for the tile themselves. They hauled it to the campus on a big trailer. All we had to buy was the grout. In the end we were able to put down a great floor that will never have to be replaced, and I got a God story that could not have been more perfect if I had planned it.

Well, in a sense I guess I did . . .

That, however, was not the only God story to come out of that renovation.

When the cafetorium building had been constructed by Citadel Bible College, it was placed on the best location on the property, on the eastern edge of Manitou Mountain with a sweeping view of the Arkansas River valley. The view was so amazing that the contractors installed a virtual glass wall along the entire east side of the structure.

What it had in vista, however, the building lacked in space for an adequate septic drain system, and the old drain field, such as it was, could not be reused. Perched on the edge of the mountain as it was, there was nowhere to place a new drain system near the building, nor was there a city sewer available on the mountain. The decision was made to install an elaborate lift-pump system that would require pumping the wastewater uphill for over one hundred yards to a grassy field on the campus.

Compounding the problem was the fact that we would have to tear up the main entrance to the YWAM campus, a boulevard style with separate entry and exit lanes divided by a row of trees and curbs. It was a striking feature as a first impression of the campus, and it would be a crying shame to tear it up, but no other option presented itself. We arranged to borrow a backhoe.

The day before we were going to cross the driveway, the Ozark city water manager, who had volunteered his time to engineer the drain system for the campus, came to look everything over. He walked with the campus director along the path the trench would take, talking together about details of the construction.

As they crossed the divider between the drives, the manager stopped abruptly and asked, "What's this?" He kicked back some leaves and grass, exposing a little square piece of plastic. "I have no idea," Jim replied.

They scraped a thin layer of dirt back and uncovered a four-inch PVC screw-in cap. They got a pipe wrench, removed the cap, and discovered a vertical piece of schedule 40 PVC pipe that went down about four feet to a horizontal pipe that obviously crossed the driveways. But there was nothing in the pipes; they were as clean as the day they had been laid some thirty years earlier, and they were directly along the route we had to follow for the septic system.

I dug up both far sides of the entry and exit lanes and found the pipe with caps on both ends. Three decades earlier, before the driveway had been placed, someone had anticipated the need to be able to cross the drive and put in the pipe with no markers or record of its location. All we had to do was slide our effluent line through the PVC pipe from one side to the other.

None of us thought it a mistake or fluke that this was exactly where we needed it to be, or that we had found it when we did. We all recognized this as the Lord's advance provision. But that was not the only provision that would come for the septic system, and this time it *was* a mistake that brought it about.

In order for the system to work properly, according to the engineered design, we had to install three 1,250-gallon concrete septic tanks in series before the lift pump. They allowed as many solids as possible to settle out so that all we were pumping to the drain field was dirty water. They would be installed in one day with a borrowed backhoe that was available only during that one day of use. It would a great deal of work for our crew to accomplish this in a single day.

We got the first hole dug just before the truck arrived with the first tank. It was then that we realized they had brought us the wrong sized tank, only a 1,000-gallon capacity. When we checked we found out that all three had been mistakenly built for us in that size. We had no choice but to keep going with the installation, but we contacted the owner of the plant where they had been made. He reviewed our order and confirmed that we had requested the larger tanks. He told us that he had an additional 1,000-gallon tank he would give us at no charge because of their mistake. But that wasn't the biggest problem we faced as a result of the error.

Each tank had to be at least six inches deeper than the previous one for the slope to use gravitational force to move the wastewater through the tanks properly. Instead of 18 inches of drop across the length of the tanks, we would now need two feet. We were digging on the edge of the top of the mountain, and we knew that if we went deep enough we were going to run into stone. We got the far side of the hole down to depth, but when the operator pulled the bucket back to the uphill side he struck stone. Fortunately, the amount was so minimal that we were able to chip it away with bars and hammer. It was inconvenient, but in the end we wound up with a better system based on the mistake.

Many people who have worked at YWAM campuses around the world have stated that we ended up with the best commercial-grade kitchen of any location, other than perhaps the main campus in Hawaii. There were several more God stories that came out of that project, for which I was grateful. This outcome was one of the hopes I'd had when I took on the renovation work—we would provide the labor, but I wanted to see God's fingerprints on it when we were done.

We delighted ourselves in the Lord, and he did indeed give us the desires of our hearts.

CHAPTER 29

He Is Able to Humble

Nebuchadnezzar was one of the greatest kings of ancient annals. Scripture tells us that God raised him up for His own purposes and glory, but all of this went to Nebuchadnezzar's head, and it was necessary for God to take the king down a peg:

> "At the end of twelve months [Nebuchadnezzar] was walking on the roof of the royal palace of Babylon, and the king answered and said, 'Is not this great Babylon, which I have built by my mighty power as a royal residence and for the glory of my majesty?' While the words were still in the king's mouth, there fell a voice from heaven, 'O King Nebuchadnezzar, to you it is spoken: The kingdom has departed from you, and you shall be driven from among men, and your dwelling shall be with the beasts of the field. And you shall be made to eat grass like an ox, and seven periods of time shall pass over you, until you know that the Most High rules the kingdom of men and gives it to whom he will.'" Daniel 4:29-32

Was it a voice that actually came from the sky? Did he hear it with his ears, or just with his mind? Scripture is not clear on this. Regardless, it came for one purpose: to show that God is able to humble even the most prideful.

At far too many points in my life than I can recall, God has had to deal with my haughty attitude. Like the prideful king, I have had in the end to exclaim, "'Now I, Nebuchadnezzar, praise and extol and honor the King of heaven, for all his works are right and his ways are just; and those who walk in pride he is able to humble'" (Daniel 4:37). Perhaps no such personal humility lesson stands out in my mind more than that one.

We had been on the YWAM Ozarks campus for less than a week as short-term staff. It was my first Monday morning staff meeting, and the campus director, Jim Nizza, was working through a list of things that needed to be done. I listened but knew that what he had to cover would not relate to the reason I was there.

At the top of that list was a note that the septic system for the primary housing dorm was malfunctioning. Making matters worse, many staff members in that building were sick. A flu bug was working its way through it, and vomiting and diarrhea were the common symptoms. It sounded as awful that morning as it does now.

I was housed in that unit but was not sick. I listened with some compassion, but it was not my concern to fix that problem. I was there to head up a building renovation project. I waited for a response from someone in the group to whom that responsibility would fall. But no one spoke.

We had moved down from the camping ministry in Michigan where I had been the maintenance person for anything technical. Phone systems, fire systems, sound systems, on campus TV, radios—all had fallen under my maintenance umbrella. As I enjoyed technical work immensely, I had been content to have it that way.

We as camp staff all shared other responsibilities as well, but one thing I avoided as much as possible was working on anything related to septic system issues. I always told myself that I didn't need one more hat to wear at camp. It was a pretty lame excuse, and the Lord was going to show me that it was a one-size-fits-all hat he wanted me to try on.

Jim talked more about the need to get the septic system going, followed by awkward silence. Some who were present knew I had a reputation for being able to work on just about anything, and pretty soon their knowledge of that fact embarrassed me into a response. I felt as though I were cornered, so I finally broke the silence, choosing my words carefully.

"Well, I really don't know much about septic systems." This was a half-truth I was hoping would get me off the hook. I didn't mention that the reason I didn't know much had been by choice. "I guess I could take a look at it."

"Great!" Jim enthused. Instead of catch-and-release, he set the hook.

He took me to where the tanks were located, and septic effluent ran out from one of the covers. Yuck. The putrid gray stream trickled off across the lawn. I thought, *Well, okay, we just need to get the tanks pumped out.* I wish . . .

It turned out it was actually the most complex septic system in the entire county. I had never seen anything like it. It was gravity fed from many separate tanks at the dorm to this two-sided collector tank and then pumped uphill to a distribution box. The box automatically balanced the flow to a complex drain field network on the other side of the hill. Jim had actually had to study to get a license to design and build the system. He literally knew more than I did at that point, but he did not understand how to troubleshoot the system.

We had the tanks pumped and discovered that someone was throwing disposable cleaning wipes into the toilets. They do not deteriorate like toilet paper. The proper filters were not in place in the tanks, and the wipes had made it down to the collection tanks, where they clogged the lift pump. I pulled the pump, cleared the debris, and it was back in service. Until the next morning.

The bathrooms were working overtime with all the sick staff, and the morning sun rose on another gray stream flowing from the lid. I suspected the pump was clogged again. We had the drain service pumper come back, empty the tanks again, and pull the effluent pump once more. But this time the situation was more serious.

We didn't anticipate that there were more of the cleaning wipes in the system. They had once again made their way into the pump, but this time the impeller of the pump had been ruined. I would have to find another and replace it.

By now there had been enough leakage around the tank lid that I had to get a big tarp, double it up, and place it up to the tank cover to lie on so I was not lying in the contaminated soil. The Arkansas sun beat on my back as I worked with my head in the smelly tank. By the end of Tuesday afternoon it was back in service. And by Wednesday morning it was out of service again.

I had wanted to be a blessing and useful in ministry at YWAM Ozarks, but by now I was frustrated. As I lay in the sun on that smelly tarp once again with my head in the septic tank, I could not stop the words from coming out of my mouth: "I didn't go to Bible school for three years to be doing this!" What I had not anticipated was a response.

Whether it was in my head, or picked up by my ears, I do not know. But what I heard was, "Really? Why not?" Not as dramatic as Nebuchadnezzar, but I knew it was the Lord, and that it was chastening time. Thankfully, God didn't make me "eat grass like an ox," although I was wondering if I had lost my mind.

I was interested in doing fun things, impressive things, popular things in my kingdom service. Give me a paper to write. Great! A message to preach? Terrific! Worship to lead? Love to. A building to renovate? No problem. But repair of septic systems didn't find a place on my bucket list of spiritual gifting or calling.

It is this inability to see pride for what it is—a cancer that drains the spiritual life from us—that makes us invalids in the kingdom, unable to address the needs of others, or even of ourselves.

Lying there on the tarp, I asked the Lord to forgive my pride and acknowledged the practical need of the YWAM staff before me. On Wednesday afternoon I discovered a new problem. The distribution box at the top of the hill had gotten plugged for the same reason as the pump. I comforted myself, knowing that after the Lord has used difficult circumstances to reprove and correct us He is free to remove them and to supply the grace we need. Wanting to move on, I fixed the box. On Thursday morning the system was inoperative again.

But that morning grace prevailed in my heart, and rather than getting frustrated I discovered that *I* was the problem. I had forgotten to turn on the power to the pump when I had finished on Wednesday. Through it all the staff were so grateful for the use of their bathrooms as the flu ran its course.

Friday morning the system was still working, and I was glad to have gotten it going, because by then I had the flu.

When the Lord whispered that thought to me at the septic tanks the tone wasn't harsh and condemning. It was soft but piercing. I had allowed a hard shell to build up around me, and I saw myself as above the humble life I needed to embrace.

When Jesus washed the feet of his disciples He was taking the humblest role in a household, one typically reserved for the lowest servant. He said to His astonished followers, "'If I . . . , your Lord and Teacher, have washed your feet, you also ought to wash one another's feet'" (John 13:14).

I can see now that one of the most important things I did at YWAM Ozarks was to fix that septic system, not because of how this ministered to the staff but because of how the process changed me.

CHAPTER 30

Home, Sweet Home

After we had finished our commitment to the YWAM Ozarks campus renovation project, we needed somewhere to live. We had nowhere else to go, so we decided to stay in Ozark and find local employment. A house for rent across the street from the church we attended was big enough for Audrey, myself, and three of our daughters.

The rent was appropriate for the house, but we knew we would have to work quickly to find a home to buy with what little we had left in the bank. Our options based on our income were pretty much limited to Veterans Administration foreclosures. A local realtor, Ray Lawless, was also on the lookout for homes we could afford.

But what we could afford was pretty discouraging. Most of the places were in rough condition or in poor locations. We submitted a few offers, but nothing came through in our favor.

One Saturday Ray had given us a house to check about ten miles north of Ozark. We finally found the house, but the location wasn't practical for us.

I had kept up optimism throughout the months while we had been looking and praying, but I'll have to say that it ran out that morning. Neither of us said much to each other as I brought Audrey back to our rental home, but I was talking to the Lord in my head. When we got to the house I told her I felt I was supposed to drive around the area looking for a "For Sale by Owner" sign in a front yard. We hadn't looked for any houses for sale by owner, in part because we thought they would all be out of our price range.

We had gotten preapproved for an $80,000 mortgage as our maximum, but that was going to be a real stretch for us. I wasn't making much where I worked, and Audrey was going to school full-time for nursing. It was the best we could do, and we would have to scrimp to make it work. But it continually seemed as though anything in that price bracket would sell before we could move on it.

I drove through areas of the community I had never been in before, looking in yard after yard, with no success. It was easy to conclude that finding a house for us to buy was just not high on the priority list for the Lord.

After about an hour of fruitless driving down street after street, I decided to return some car parts that I didn't need to a parts store back north of town where we had been earlier in the day. As I rolled to a stop at the street it was on, there was quite a gathering of cars (15-20) around a house and in its yard directly across from me. Some kind of family gathering, I assumed. I rounded the corner and drove to the parts store.

But on the way back I noticed that every car that had been in front of that house was now gone, and in their place was a "For Sale by Owner" sign. I could hardly believe it. In all the months we had been looking for a house, not once had I seen a "For Sale by Owner" sign in a yard in Ozark. I parked, and with no one home I walked around the house. It seemed ideal. It was the perfect size, and located almost exactly in the middle between where I worked, where Audrey attended nursing school classes, and Jo's high school.

There was no price on the sign, but there was a phone number, so I called it immediately. The seller told me someone had already called and was going to go to a bank to try to arrange for financing. Whoever came up with the money had first shot. I said I was already approved, had a cash down payment of several thousand dollars, and asked about the price.

The elderly homeowner had died, and the daughter told me they wanted only $80,000 so they could sell the house quickly. The bank approved the purchase, and we started the process.

We closed on the house on the day Audrey started Christmas break, and we moved the last box in on the last day before she had to go back to school. We weren't totally unpacked, but we were home.

It had been 27 years since we had owned a home of our own. It allowed us to be with our oldest daughter and her husband in Ozark and see four of their children born there.

Dorothy of *The Wizard of Oz* had it right. "There's no place like home."

CHAPTER 31

Now Is the Time

My wife and I purchased that home in December of 2010. We knew up front that this investment was going to be a financial stretch. But a few months later, when a mortgage payment came due, we found ourselves already in financial trouble. Technically we had enough income, but the way the timing of bills worked out, one month meant that we would miss the date for the house payment, and it was too late to rearrange the due dates.

I had purchased an old, used pickup truck in really nice shape from a brother in Christ in our church family. I was able to buy it cheap because it hadn't run in a while, but with some TLC I was able to get it going. We were going to need it because the house we had bought had a fireplace, and we would need a way to haul firewood, as we were planning to supplement our heating system by using it to hold down our winter bills. We began to passionately ask the Lord for wisdom with relation to our financial crisis.

One of the most important aspects of developing a prayer life that gets answers is an unselfish attitude. That does not mean we do not pray for things. It means that as we pray we are seeking to factor in what God wants, not just what we want—as Jesus prayed in the garden, "'If it is possible, let this cup pass from me; nevertheless, not as I will, but as you will'" (Matthew 26:39).

After a couple of stressful weeks anticipating the inevitable, I finally reached the decision that I had to seriously consider selling my truck. But I didn't want to run ahead of or lag behind what the Lord was doing in our lives. I fasted with prayer, waiting for what I could consider a clear indication of what I should do. I did not want to be like King Saul, who let his circumstances and human reason dictate his decision to offer a sacrifice, as opposed to trusting God.

I reached what I considered a crucial moment in the process of seeking God's guidance on our finances. There was simply no time left. As I drove into my driveway on the third day, I prayed, "Father, I have to hear from you on this now. I am willing to sell the truck, though I don't know how you will provide later when we need it. But do I wait to sell it, or do I sell it now? What do I do?"

I went in the living room to my favorite prayer place. As I began to pray, I remembered a sister in Christ in Georgia, Mechelle Green. She had often had an impact in my life by sharing things from the Lord—Scriptures, devotionals, and messages she had heard or read—oftentimes exactly what I needed when I needed it. I hadn't talked to her in months but felt I should call her.

She was just about to leave the house for an appointment and hesitated to answer the phone. But she sensed that she needed to take the call, and we talked briefly about what had been going on in her life during that time. She'd had an extended struggle with illness and yet had a glowing testimony of trust in the Lord. I hoped she would say something that might be from the Lord to help me in my decision, but I decided not to tell her what was going on or what I had prayed minutes earlier.

I could sense that she needed to get off the phone, so I let the call wind down and accepted that this would not be the answer to my prayer. We were about to hang up when I heard her suddenly catch her breath and say, "The Holy Spirit says, 'Now is the time.'"

I was stunned.

This was exactly what I had to hear. No more, no less. She had absolutely no idea what I was facing, or what I had asked God to say to me. Joy flooded my soul as I told her what had just happened, not just because of what it meant to me but because of what it meant to her on the other end of the phone as she erupted in praise to God. But the answer was bigger than either of us realized at the moment.

I went out to buy "For Sale" signs that evening in immediate obedience to what I believed God had said to me. As I did, I had the sudden awareness that maybe selling the truck involved more than just my need for cash. Maybe there was someone who needed a good truck, and this would be the answer to their prayer as well. I got at least ten phone calls in 24 hours, but one guy in particular called from my church.

His son had been in detention for drug abuse and was about to be released. The father had been looking for a truck to help his son be able to work and get a fresh start in life. I told him that many others had called, so he came to the house early to wait for me to get home from work. As he waited, someone else arrived ten minutes later. But he said he got the sense that this was meant to be. He drove the truck, and it was exactly what he was looking for. He gave me what I asked—and gave his son another shot at getting his life straightened out.

The sale gave us enough to cover the house payment, plus some extra for the bills. We would come up with a way to get firewood. But with the way I had received direction from the Lord, I knew it would work out.

It is impossible that my friend in Georgia of her own accord could have said exactly the four words I needed to hear ("The Holy Spirit says . . ."), since I had given her absolutely no indication of what was going on in my life or mentioned my prayer. We live hundreds of miles apart. But then, distance isn't an issue. We do have a common friend, don't we? And He knew exactly what I needed to hear.

CHAPTER 32

All These Things

Jesus instructed his disciples, "'Do not lay up for yourselves treasures on earth, where moth and rust destroy and where thieves break in and steal'" (Matthew 6:19). Does this mean that we cannot or should not ask God for specific material things?

There is actually a word play going on in the verse in the original language. The Greek underlying the words "lay up" is *thēsaurizō*, which means to store up, heap up, or accumulate more than you actually need. The word rendered "treasures" is *thēsauros*. Notice the shared Greek root. The verse could be translated, "Don't treasure up treasures." The context is clearly an emphasis on not being consumed with stockpiling the objects of your desires, as the world is, but trusting in God to give you what you need when you need it.

The attitude of a disciple is contrasted with those of the world who spend their time and energy chasing after the desires, or treasures, of their flesh. Jesus warned them, "'Where your treasure is, there your heart will be also'" (Matthew 6:21). It is a case not of having things, but of things having you. You cannot serve two masters.

After we had sold our truck, we made do getting wood for the fireplace, hauling a few armloads in our car at a time, but it was difficult. I had to rely on my son-in-law, Josh, to haul loads to my house when we went out to cut together—which wasn't all that bad an arrangement.

I had been in charge of firewood production at the camp where we had been on staff. Every summer for many years I would take crews of teenage guys out to harvest dead trees for the many fireplaces and furnaces on the camp. Although it sounds like an awful amount of work, and it was, this was an activity I really enjoyed with the guys. Some of them had never done work as hard as that, and it became a rite of passage for them. It was time for Josh and me to be together as well.

But the beat up old four-wheel-drive truck he had was pretty iffy. For instance, when you put it in park, you still sometimes had to put something behind a wheel to make sure it wouldn't roll away. It was in such rough condition I hated to ask him to drive it to my house. I really needed another truck of my own.

A few years earlier I had run across a true "barn find" motorcycle, a 1981 Kawasaki 750 four cylinder, and was able to buy it for $450. It needed cleaning up, and some very minor repair, but in no time I had a totally original vintage bike with less than 3,500 miles on it in beautiful condition. Guys would stop me to talk about it, and three times I had been offered $2,000, but I wasn't interested in selling.

By the time I was sixty, though, I really didn't have time for or interest in riding it; during the last year I'd had it I had ridden it only twice. I decided I needed to put the bike up for sale and see whether I could find a used truck.

We were in a perfect location to sell it, on a city section of a main highway with lots of traffic. The "Pig Trail," as it is known, is one of the premier motorcycle routes in Arkansas, and hundreds of motorcycle riders pass our house every summer. My motorcycle was a real eye-catcher, and it ran like a watch. Though lots of guys agreed it was worth the money I was asking, no one who stopped was interested in giving me that much. But it was the only thing I could sell that would give me a shot at getting money for a truck. Even then, for $2,000, I didn't expect much of a truck.

I was mowing the lawn one day and started wondering if I should drop the price and take whatever I could get for it. I remembered the time I had been mowing the yard three decades earlier and had stopped to pray about selling our house to go to school. That had worked once, so why not try again?

I throttled down the mower and stopped in the middle of the yard to pray, people again driving by as they had many years earlier. I asked the Lord for wisdom. Should I reduce the price or hold out for what I was asking? I had already narrowed down what I hoped to get for a truck—a 2000-2004 two-wheel-drive Ford F150, with a V6 4.2 liter engine for good gas mileage, and a short box to turn tight in the woods, with around one hundred thousand miles on it—and I talked to the Lord about it. Again, I have learned to pray for exactly what I need in order that I might clearly see the Lord's stamp of approval on what I was seeking. I ended my prayer asking for whatever would bring Him glory, whether that meant getting what I was asking for the bike or reducing the price and seeing Him provide some other way to meet my need.

I throttled the mower back up and went back to mowing, though I didn't yet have a sense of whether or not to reduce the price. My yard still needed mowing, regardless of that answer.

About a half hour later I had just put the mower away when a guy on a really nice, newer motorcycle pulled up to look at my bike. His was obviously worth a lot more than mine, so I anticipated another conversation with someone who had just stopped to admire my Kawasaki. But not so.

He had borrowed a motorcycle from a friend who was on another bike, and this guy wanted one of his own. He loved mine, and after looking it over and listening to it purr, he asked whether I was interested only in selling it or would consider a trade?

I told him I really had to get what I was asking because I needed to buy a truck. His eyes lit up. He had a truck he would be interested in trading. I asked what he had.

He had a 2000 two-wheel-drive Ford F150, V6 4.2 liter, short box, with one hundred thirty thousand miles. I could hardly believe it. It was exactly what I had described to the Lord in prayer thirty minutes earlier. "But," he added, "It's in really good shape and runs great. I would have to have more than $2,000 for it." I was afraid I was seeing the deal slip out of reach. "What would you need for it?" I asked.

"$3,000," was his firm response. I didn't have another $1,000, but I did have another option.

"I have an older Toyota Camry I am planning to sell. If you can wait, I think I could come up with the cash pretty quickly. I hope to get $1,000 for it." Again, the guy's eyes lit up. "You have a car too?" He told me he would trade his truck for both the motorcycle and the car.

I would have felt the Lord had answered my prayer if I had gotten half of the specifics I had asked for. But *all* of them? What were the odds of a guy at random pulling up into my driveway a half hour after I had asked the Lord for exactly the truck he had available for trade, and of my having exactly what he was looking for in a motorcycle and car, worth exactly what he needed to have for his truck?

It is hard to recall this story without remembering these verses from James: "You do not have, because you do not ask. You ask and do not receive, because you ask wrongly, to spend it on your passions" (James 4:2–3).

I was once astonished to hear a Pentecostal pastor rev up a congregation in prayer for a new Cadillac. The pastor tried to use prayer authority to cause a glitch in the computers of a local bank, depositing enough money in the pastor's bank account to cover the cost. I can confidently say that prayer got a heavenly response of No!

I hadn't asked the Lord for a new truck, or even an impressive used vehicle—just what I needed to get wood hauled and work done around our house. But again, what I wanted and asked for most of all is to bring glory to the Lord, subject to His will for my life in His kingdom. That is what Jesus taught His disciples was to be the foundation of their prayer life.

CHAPTER 33

Bad Dreams and a Wounded Soldier

It was dark. Bill was struggling to subdue his attacker, a Viet Cong soldier. Bill was an Army sniper in Vietnam, one of the best, but somehow—he wasn't sure why—he had encountered a soldier on the ground.

Bill wrestled his way on top of the soldier and brought the weight of his body down on his enemy, whom he now had by the throat. He would take him out the hard way instead of with a rifle.

Then Bill woke up.

He was in bed on top of his wife, Cheryl, choking her. He fell to her side, and they both lay there terrified. Every night for forty years since he had left Vietnam, Bill had experienced nightmares of being back in the jungle. Every. Night.

"It got to the point," Cheryl said, "where we didn't know what to do. We thought maybe we would have to sleep in separate rooms and lock the doors."

I had been acquainted with Bill, basically by name only, since we attended the same church, First Baptist in Ozark, Arkansas. I offered to lead a men's Bible study fellowship, and one night I spoke on forgiveness to the guys, including Bill.

In the Bible study I was really focused on forgiving others for their wrongs toward us, when Bill put his hand up and caught me unprepared with his question. "What do you do," he asked, "when you can't forgive yourself?"

"I need a little more information," I responded, really just stalling for time to come up with some kind of appropriate answer for him. "What do you mean by not being able to forgive yourself?"

Bill started to go into some of his background as a soldier, and I could see that it was going to take some time to get a solid grasp on where he was mentally and what had led to that question. I asked him to stay after the Bible study was finished, and I would talk to him then.

After the others had left, he related his war experience as one of the top ten snipers in the Army at the time, and how he had struggled with nightmares ever since he had left Vietnam. Even after he had finished active duty, he had been involved in covert operations, and later in law enforcement. He talked about his reality of not being able to forgive himself for what those responsibilities had sometimes required of him. He explained what was happening in his home with his wife, and the constant cloud of fear that was beginning to envelop them.

As he spoke to me I was asking the Lord to show me what I needed to say to Bill, to give him hope and to bring about healing in his life. I had never encountered anyone with his life experiences. Listening to his anguish, I began to understand the foundational truths that Bill needed to accept and apply to his life from Scripture.

I walked him through verses related to his identity in Christ and showed him in Romans 12 that there are actually those who "bear the sword" as part of their divine calling to serve others and protect them. Bill had not gone out to selfishly kill people—just to fulfill his orders as a soldier.

I suspected that there could be another dimension involved behind the nightmares, a spiritual one. I remembered the repeated interruption of my sleep I mentioned earlier in the book. Again,

Revelation 12:17 teaches that Satan occupies himself by making war against the Lamb and His followers. Lest anyone misunderstand, let me be quick to say that I do not blame all nightmares on demons. But in seeking to bring relief to this wounded warrior I did not want to leave any stone unturned. If this were not simply a case of assuaging a guilty conscience after the violence of war, I was going to try to be sure the one who declared war on the people of God did not get a free ride on this one.

There was another interesting dimension to this situation. Bill's spiritual gift was evangelism. It would be easy to see why the devil would want to bring destruction and despair to the life of someone with that gift.

Most Christians tragically know little to nothing about the reality of spiritual warfare against believers. I gave Bill a list of verses to read on forgiveness and identity in Christ just before he went to bed, five times each to help them stick in his mind more effectively. I told him that if Christ had forgiven him, he had to forgive himself as well, or he was negating what Christ had done on his behalf. Instead of five repetitions, he read them ten times each.

Bill's own spiritual gifting seemed to me to be part of his healing and protection. I said, "Before you go to bed, I want you to write down the names of six world leaders you don't believe are Christians. Make a list of those names and put them on the nightstand by your bed. If you are awakened in the night with another nightmare, I want you to get on your knees and pray fervently for the salvation of all those leaders. You are an evangelist, and your prayers for them will be powerful. I believe that if these nightmares are an attack of Satan on you, they will cease." Instead of six names he came up with twelve, and laid the paper on the nightstand before he lay his head on the pillow.

Bill woke up abruptly. The list was on the nightstand. But just as suddenly he realized it was morning, and he had slept through the night for the first time in forty years without a nightmare.

He was free of them, and night after night he and Cheryl slept without fear.

Astonished at the immediacy of his recovery, I was embarrassed to ask him whether he'd had any more of the nightmares. But I casually did so every couple of weeks until I could see he was getting frustrated by what would have appeared to be my own lack of faith. I just wanted to be sure there were no lingering effects to deal with. After a few months I stopped asking.

Bill was so shocked by what had happened that he immediately began to reach out to veterans to share what Jesus had done in his life—and could do in theirs.

There is an interesting compound Greek term, *metanoia*, which I think is far more relevant to mental and spiritual freedom and healing than we realize. It is most often interpreted as "repentance" in the New Testament, but it literally translates as change (*meta*) mind (*noia*). I often like to refer to it as healing of the mind. The apostle Paul used it in 2 Timothy:

> "The Lord's servant must not be quarrelsome but kind to everyone, able to teach, patiently enduring evil, correcting his opponents with gentleness. God may perhaps grant them repentance [*metanoia*] leading to a knowledge of the truth, and they may come to their senses and escape from the snare of the devil, after being captured by him to do his will." 2 Timothy 2:24-26

Here the apostle identifies *metanoia* as a gift from God that leads to understanding the truth about themselves, sin, and even God Himself. That results in people coming to their senses and escaping from Satan's oppressive control, a control that might otherwise have destroyed them and those around them. That destruction is what almost happened with Bill and Cheryl.

It was understanding and applying truth that led to Bill's freedom. In his case it was the psychological injury he had brought back from Vietnam that plagued him and nearly destroyed their marriage. Was there a spiritual dimension of oppression involved as well? I think that is possible, but we will never know for certain.

Bill and Cheryl moved away from the area, so I have been unable to verify that he is still nightmare free. Applying scriptural truth to our lives to gain freedom is not a one-time event, however. It is an ongoing process that we need to practice consistently. This is true even of the spiritual aspect of freedom and cleansing.

Jesus taught an important truth on this aspect of spiritual healing:

> "'When the unclean spirit has gone out of a person, it passes through waterless places seeking rest, and finding none it says, 'I will return to my house from which I came.' And when it comes, it finds the house swept and put in order. Then it goes and brings seven other spirits more evil than itself, and they enter and dwell there. And the last state of that person is worse than the first.'" Luke 11:24–26

If we do not continue to walk in truth, whether truth of our identity in Christ or of our spiritual victory over the powers of darkness, we can end up worse off than we started.

Conclusion

There you have it. I am no one special; I haven't walked on water or led any mass crusades. I am as "plain Jane" as a Christian gets. But I wouldn't trade the past four decades of relationship with the Lord for anything else anyone could offer.

After reading these true stories from my life and walk with the Lord, you might find that you have more questions than answers. Good. Remember that this one of the things I said I hoped would happen. But in another sense, I have to say *Join the club!*

Why didn't God answer your prayers for a dying child, an alcoholic spouse, or a job when yours ran out and you lost your home? Why doesn't He answer prayers of people who are followers of other faiths? I am going to admit that I don't have answers to all of the questions that could arise from what I have shared with you. I don't know you or your circumstances.

I can only say that as I have read the Bible and applied it to my life as a disciple of Jesus, what you have read, and much more that I did not have room to include, was the result.

But let me ask you a couple of questions that may not have occurred to you.

First, what difference would it make in your life to understand that God truly knows your thoughts and hears your words? I have offered evidence from my own life of that reality, stories that defy any other explanation. We will someday give account for our thoughts, words, and deeds.

Second, have you ever considered the lengths to which God has gone in order to have a personal relationship with you? He even delivered up His own Son to death on a cross to make that possible.

To that end God redeemed us by the blood of Jesus, offered us spiritual life by the indwelling Holy Spirit, delegated authority to us in the name of Jesus over the powers of darkness, restored to us dominion over His Creation, and entrusts us with the responsibility of calling others to become part of the kingdom of the Messiah.

He has given us the awesome privilege of approaching Him with our requests and seeing answered prayer, sometimes instantaneously.

But third, the Lord made the kind of interactive promises I have written about to apply only to His relationship with disciples, those who have yielded themselves to walking with Him and seeking first His kingdom. You might attend church, but are you a disciple? Might that lack of connection explain why God seems distant and aloof from your life?

At one time I had become a "none," unimpressed by a theoretical God and a religious system that made no difference in my life. But no longer. After all I have seen, heard, and touched related to the kingdom of God, I could never have enough faith to believe it is fantasy, that there is no God, or that genuine Christianity is a made-up belief system to assuage the fear of death in man—or simply as a means to control them.

The call to follow Jesus is God's extraordinary invitation to ordinary people. There is absolutely no reason why anyone else cannot have the same type of engagement with God as I have had, and continue to have after four decades. I am no one special.

I just love to collect beautiful stones, and share them with others, whether they are my grandchildren, or friends, or even total strangers. And now I have shared my pile of memorial stones with you.

He is there. He is real. He answers prayer. I found the desire of my heart. I hope you do too.